A Degas Sketchbook

THE HALÉVY SKETCHBOOK, 1877–1883

by EDGAR DEGAS

DOVER PUBLICATIONS, INC.
NEW YORK

PUBLISHER'S NOTE

The drawings on the following pages were done in a sketchbook at the home, on the Rue de Douai, Paris, of Ludovic Halévy (1834–1908), nephew of the composer Fromental Halévy (1799–1862) and noted opera and operetta librettist (frequently working in collaboration with Henri Meilhac). According to Daniel Halévy, Ludovic's son, Degas would draw in the book during evening gatherings to make studies for works on canvas (such as *Miss Lala at the Cirque Fernando*), to record something that had happened during the day, to render the works of others (such as the Cézanne bather) for discussion or simply to keep his hand in motion during conversation.

Many familiar themes appear here—singers at the café-concert, ballerinas, laundresses. Not all the sketches are by Degas. Several are identified on the page as the work of the composer Ernest Reyer: two portraits of Degas and those of Halévy and Ernest Guiraud (composer of the recitatives to Bizet's *Carmen* and editor of *Les Contes d'Hoffmann* by Offenbach—himself depicted in a witty sketch).

By 1883, Degas was sufficiently worried about his worsening eyesight to abandon making these evening sketches. In 1888, when Degas' illustrations for Halévy's *Les Petites Cardinal* met with the author's lack of enthusiasm, the friendship cooled; when the two took opposing views of the Dreyfus Affair, it ended.

This Dover edition, first published in 1988, is a republication of *Edgar Degas/Album de Dessins*, originally published by Quatre Chemins-Editart, Paris, 1949, in an edition limited to 550 copies. The introduction to that edition (appearing in a separate brochure), written by Daniel Halévy, is here omitted, and the plates have been rearranged for reasons of space.

Manufactured in the United States of America
Dover Publications, Inc., 31 East 2nd Street, Mineola, N.Y. 11501

Library of Congress Cataloging-in-Publication Data

Degas, Edgar, 1834–1917.
A Degas sketchbook.

Previously published as: Album de dessins. 1949.
1. Degas, Edgar, 1834–1917—Themes, motives.
2. Halévy, Ludovic, 1834–1908—Notebooks, sketchbooks, etc. I. Title.
NC248.D38A4 1989 741.944 88-31010
ISBN 0-486-25926-9

Tous les dessins de cet album sont de Degas —

Ludovic Halévy

1877 et années suivantes /

Il y en a deux ou trois de [illegible] le [illegible] —

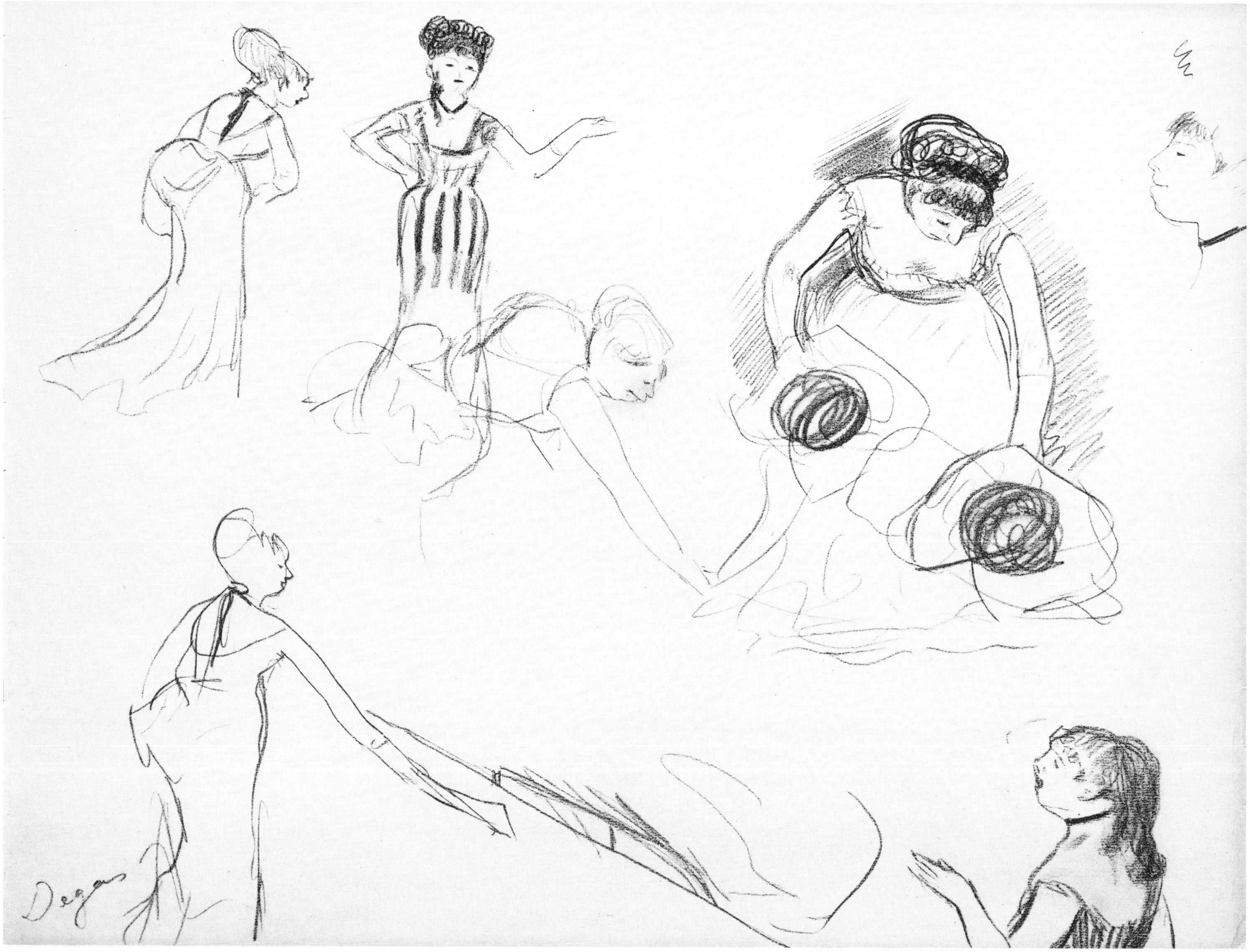
Degas

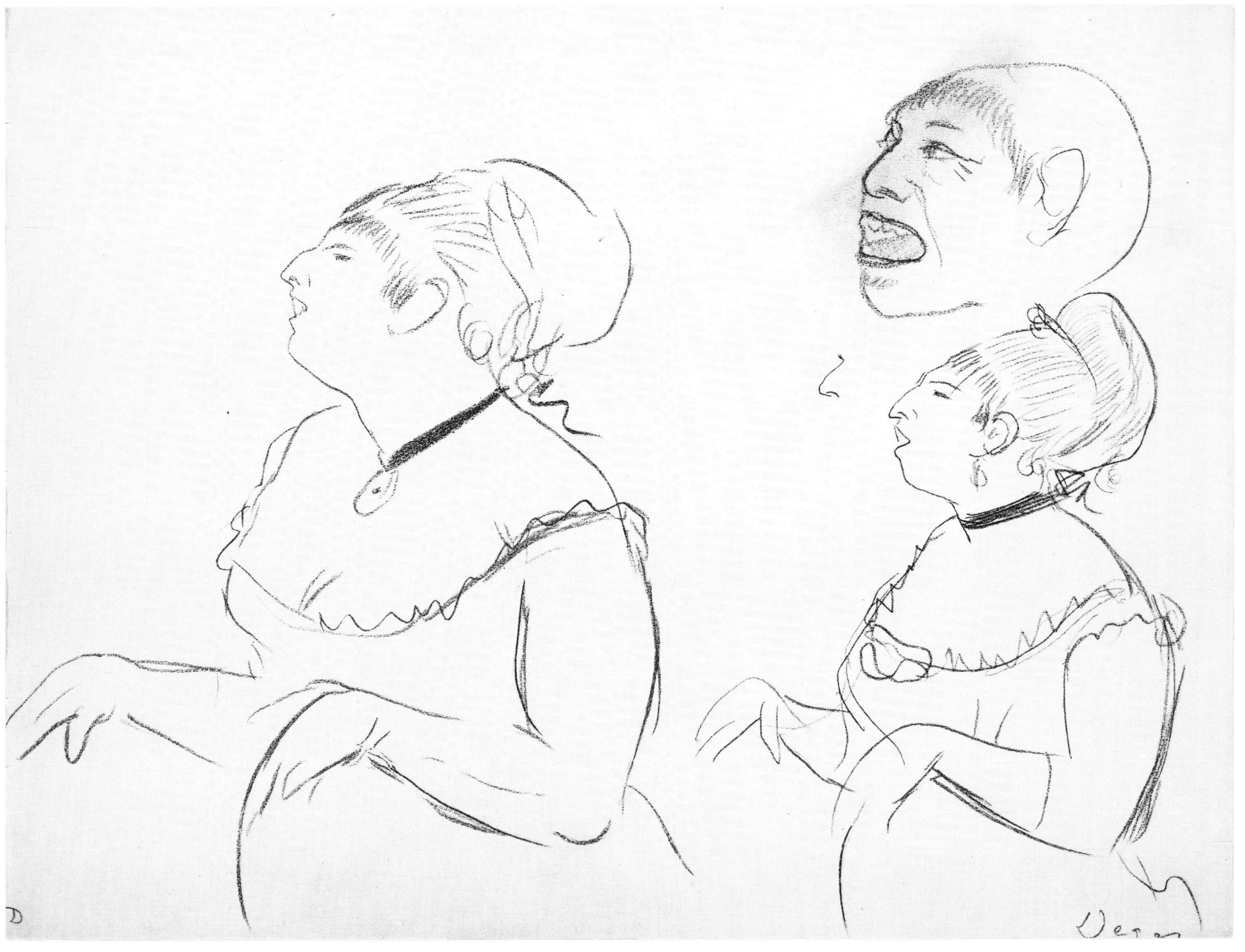

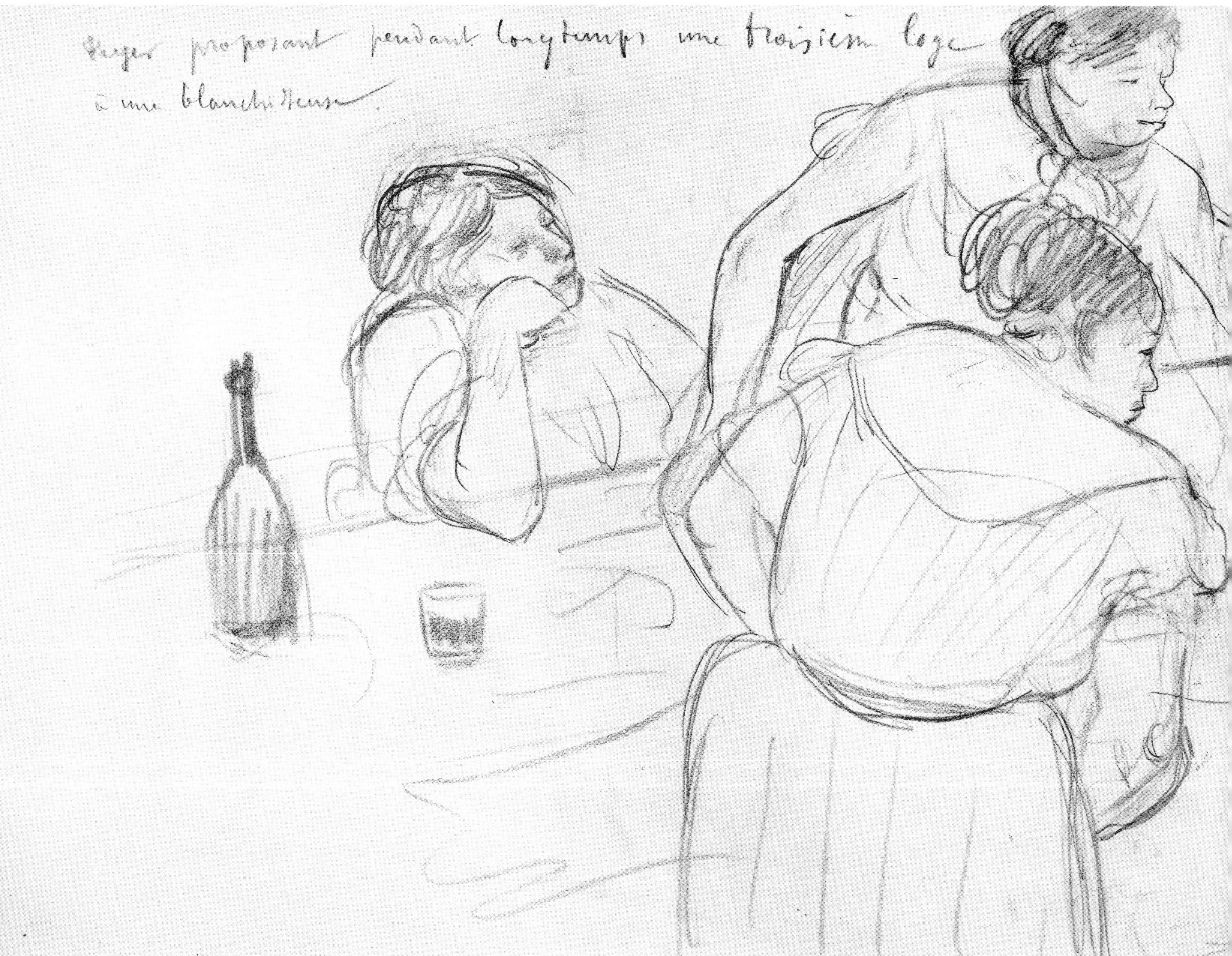
Reyer proposant pendant longtemps une troisiem loge
à une blanchisseuse

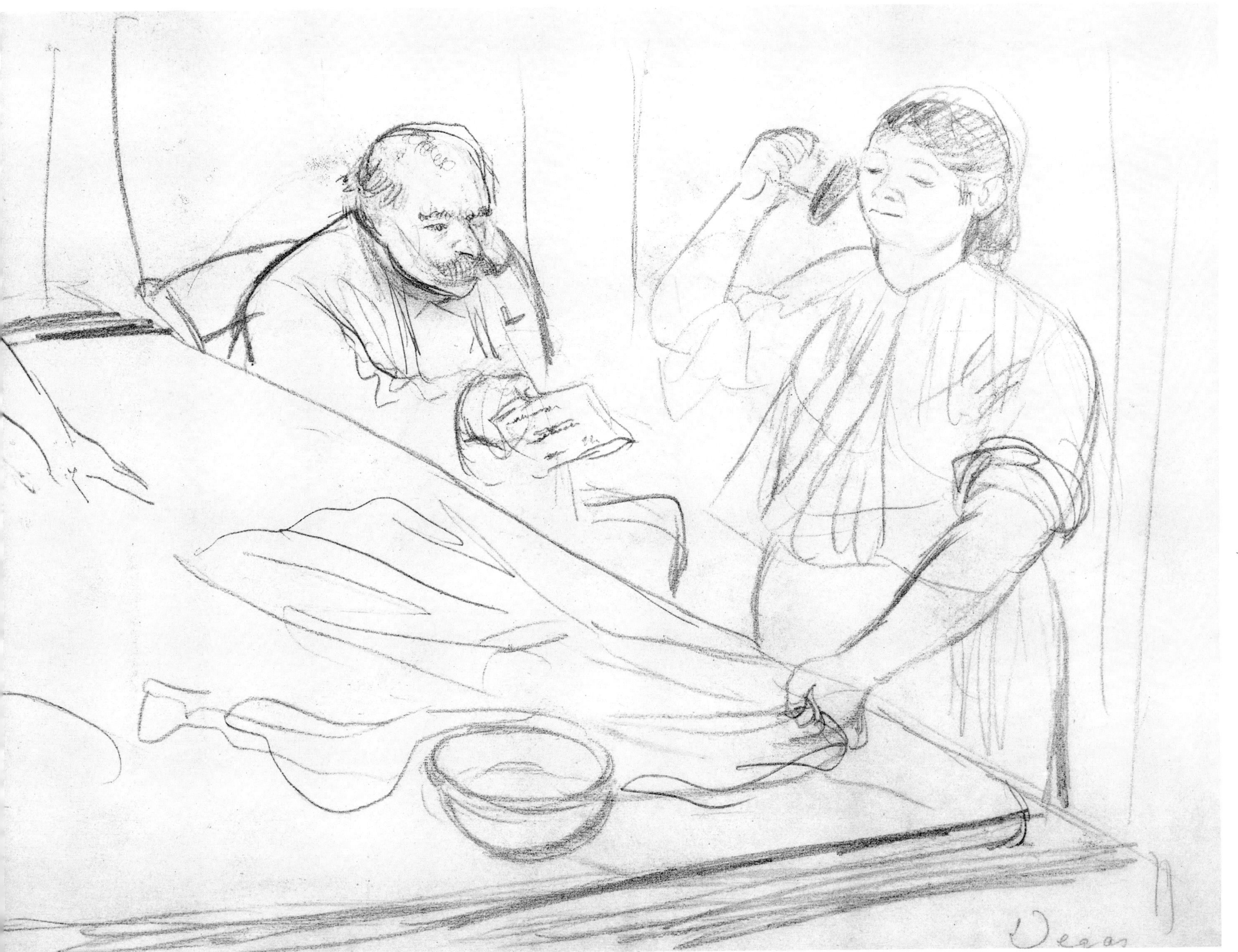
Degas

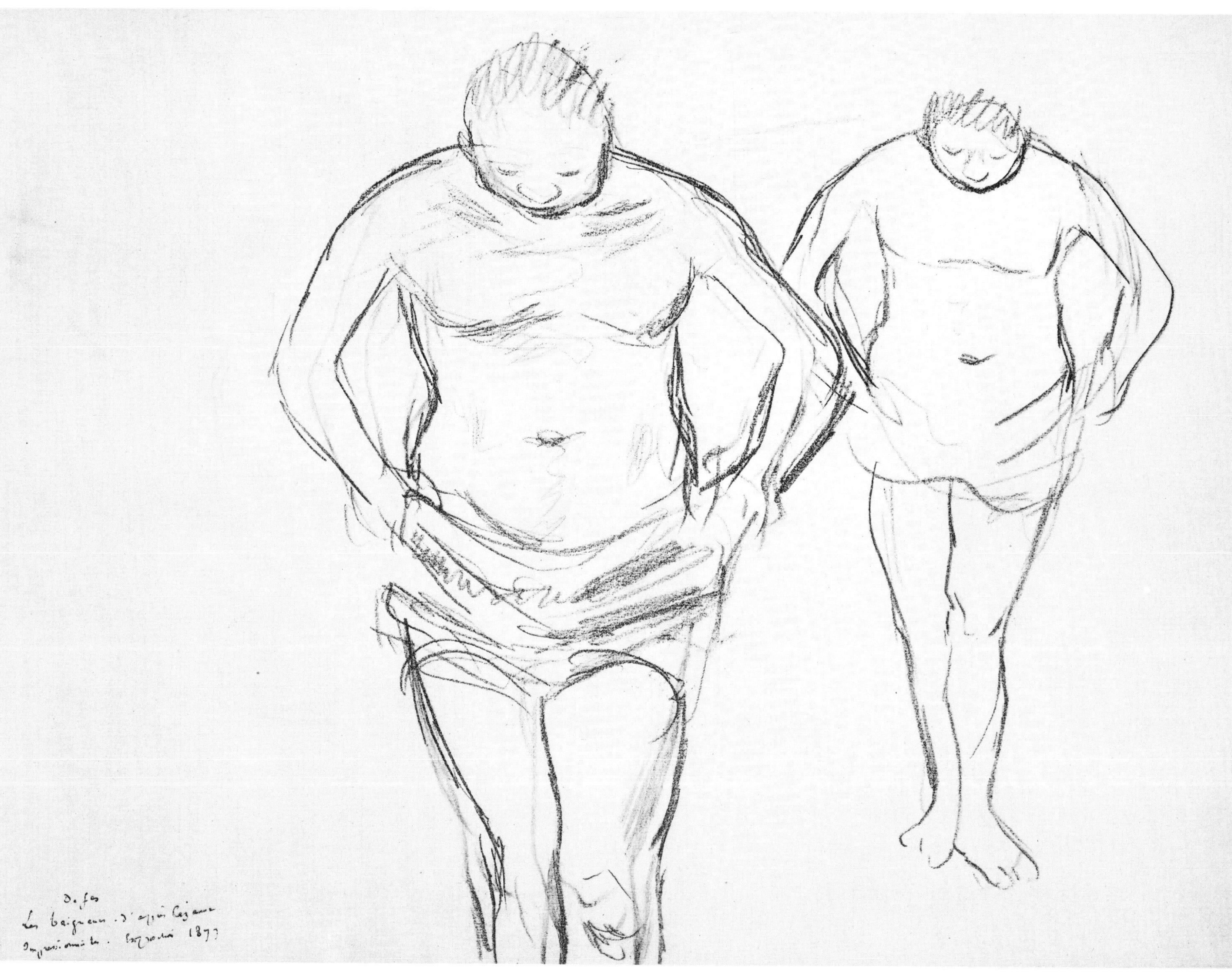

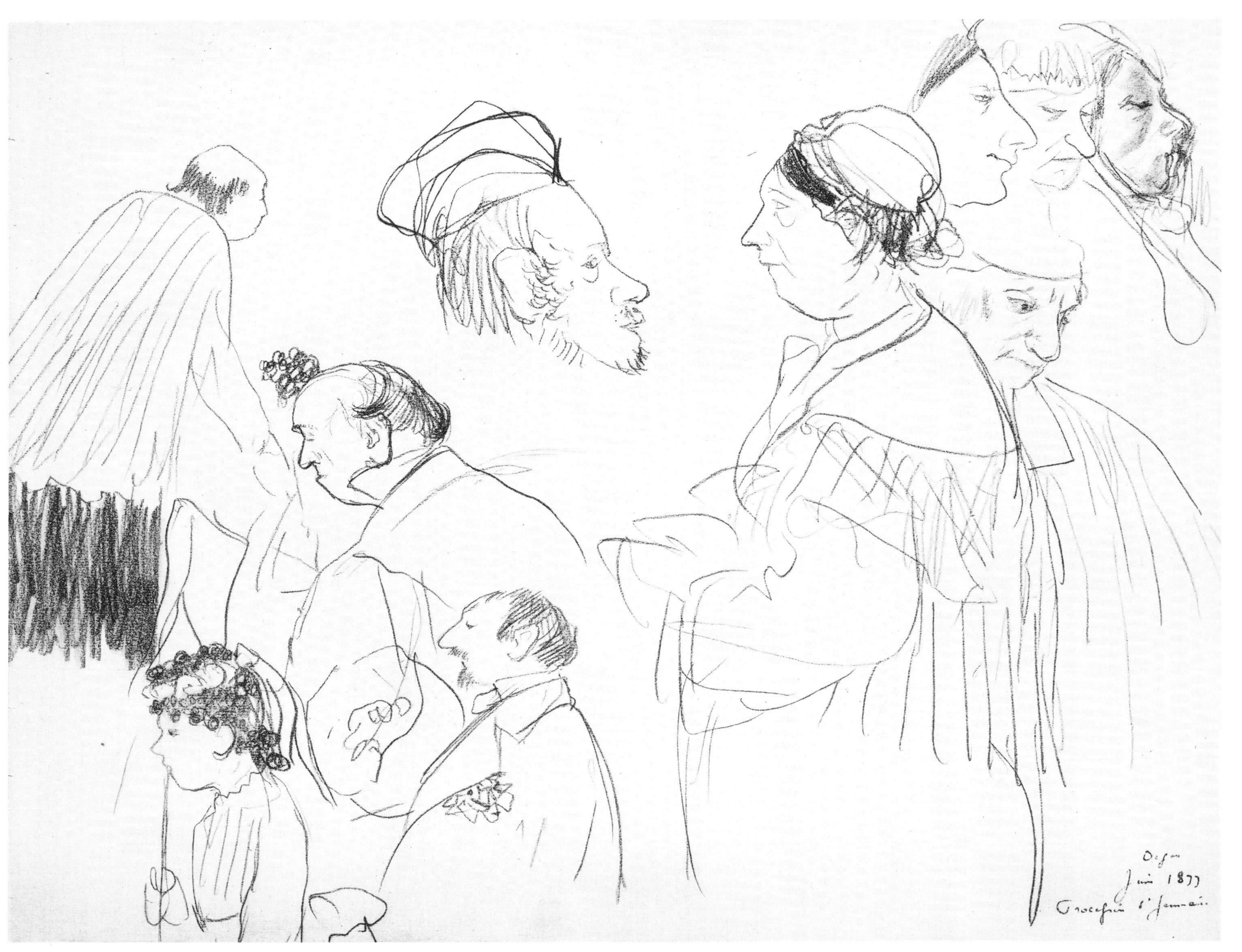
Degas
Juin 1877

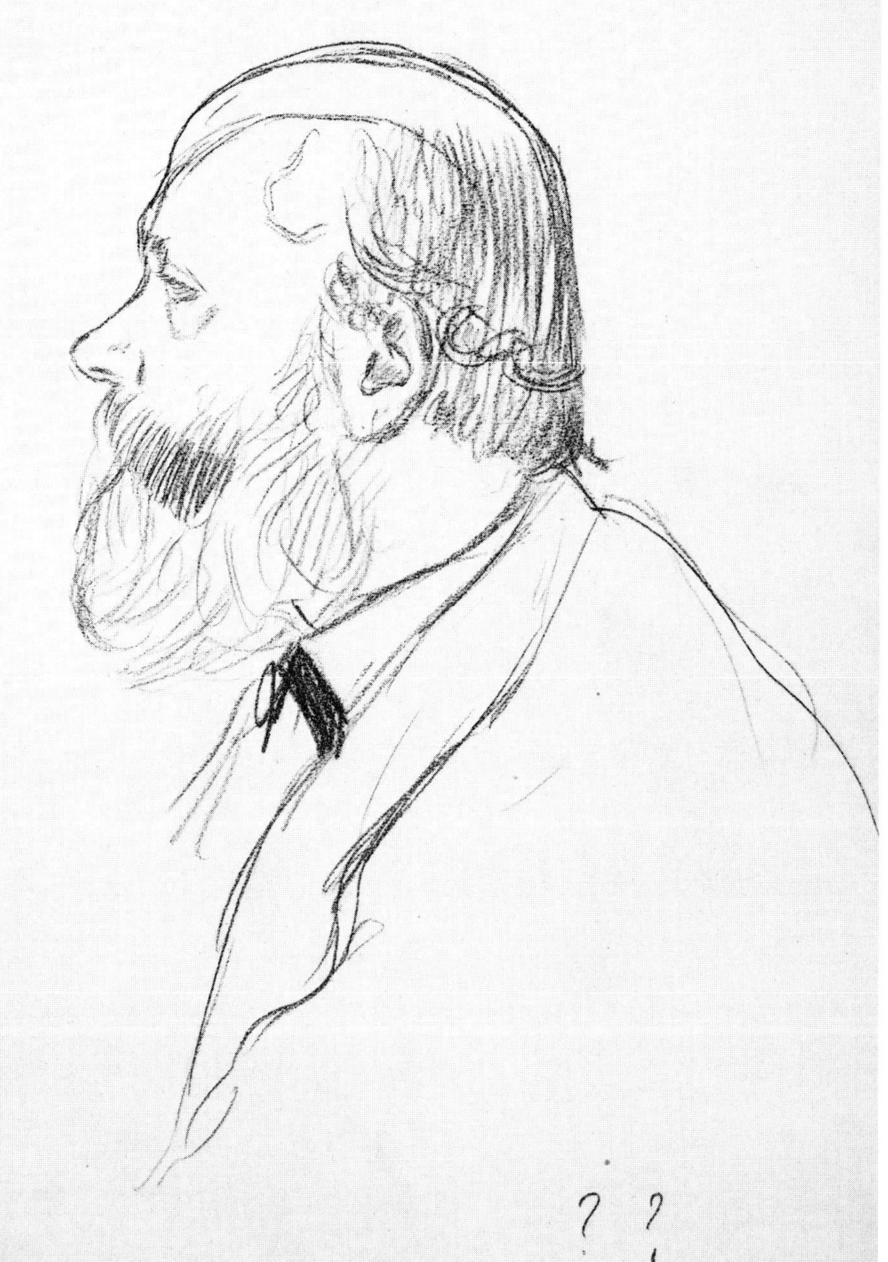

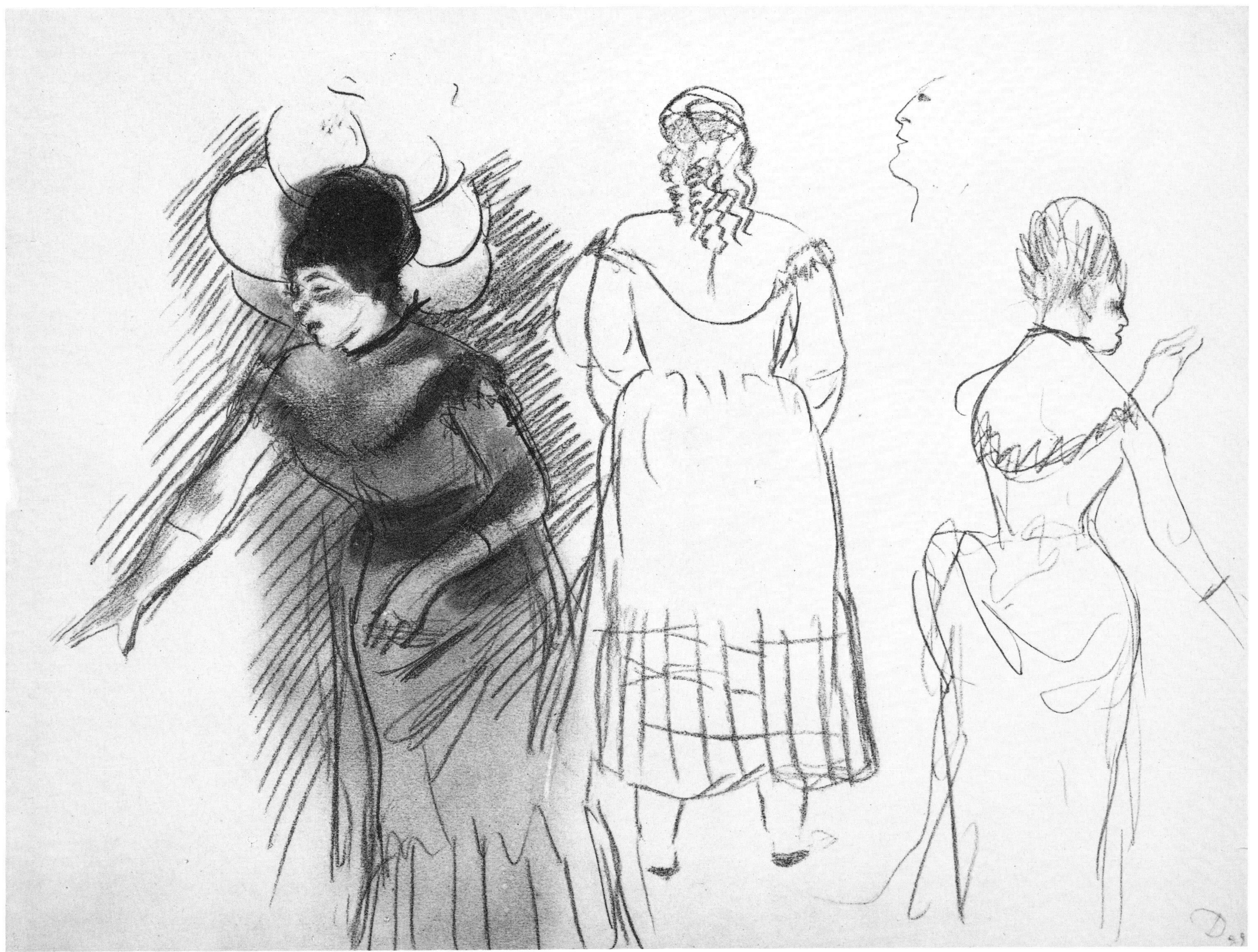

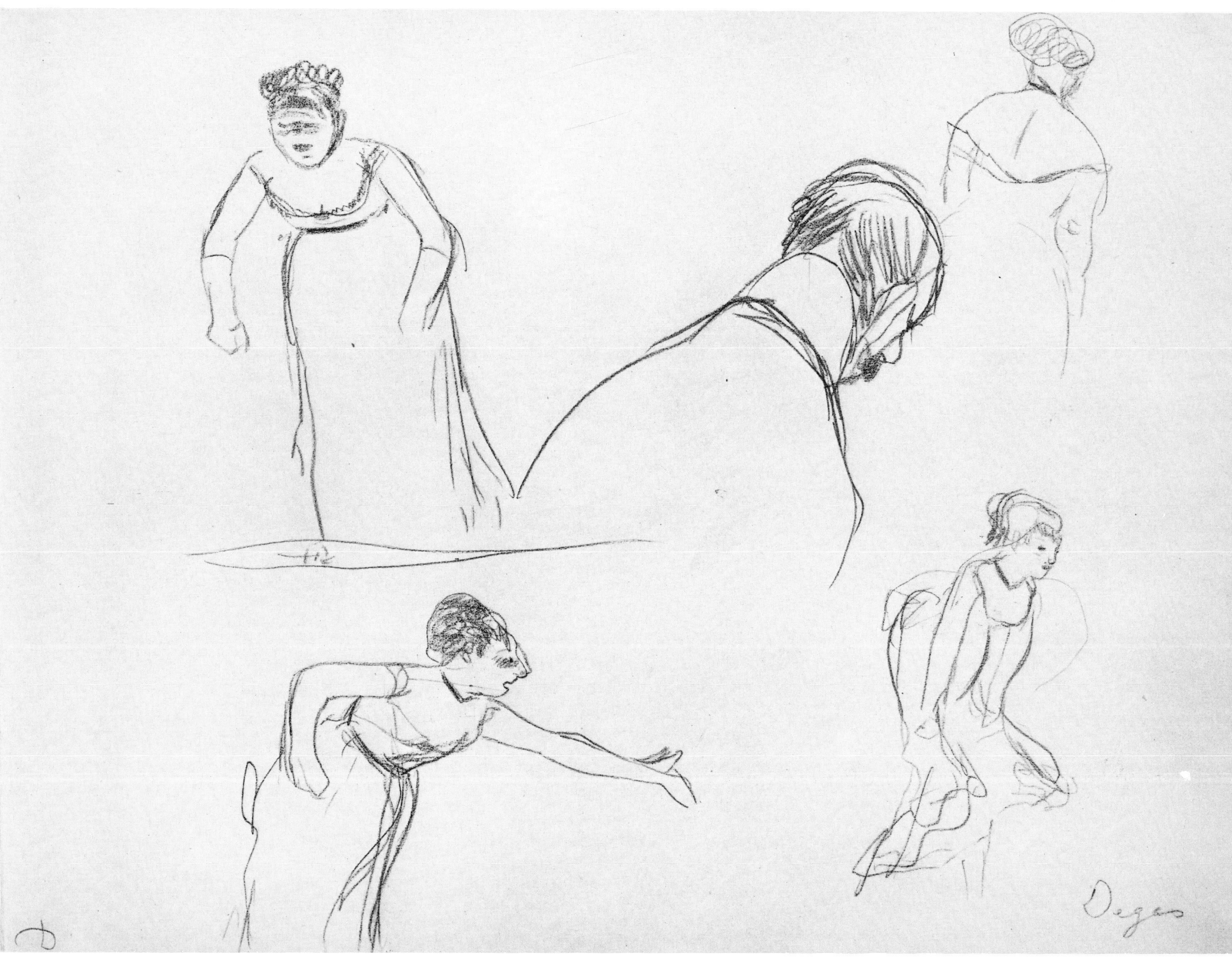
Degas

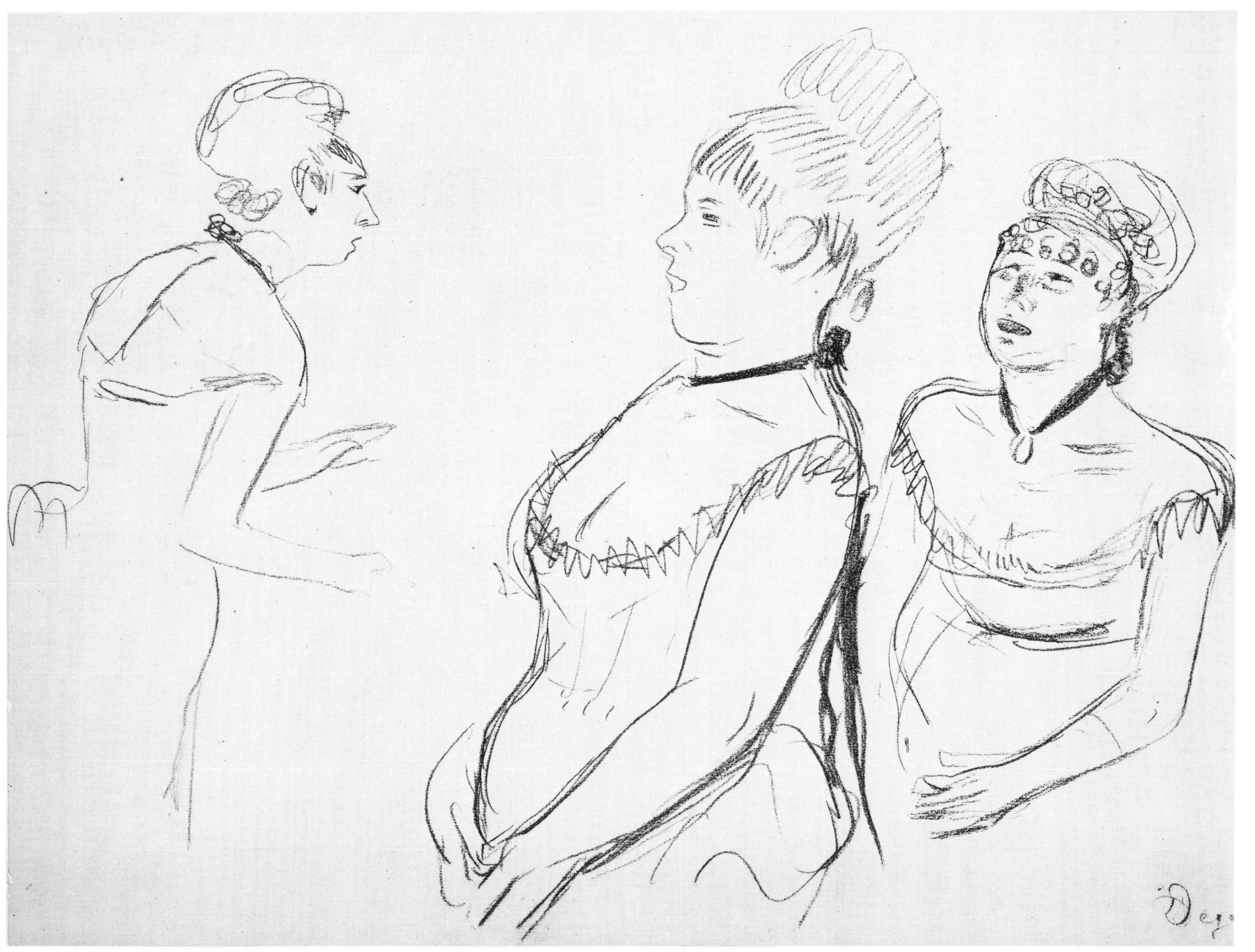

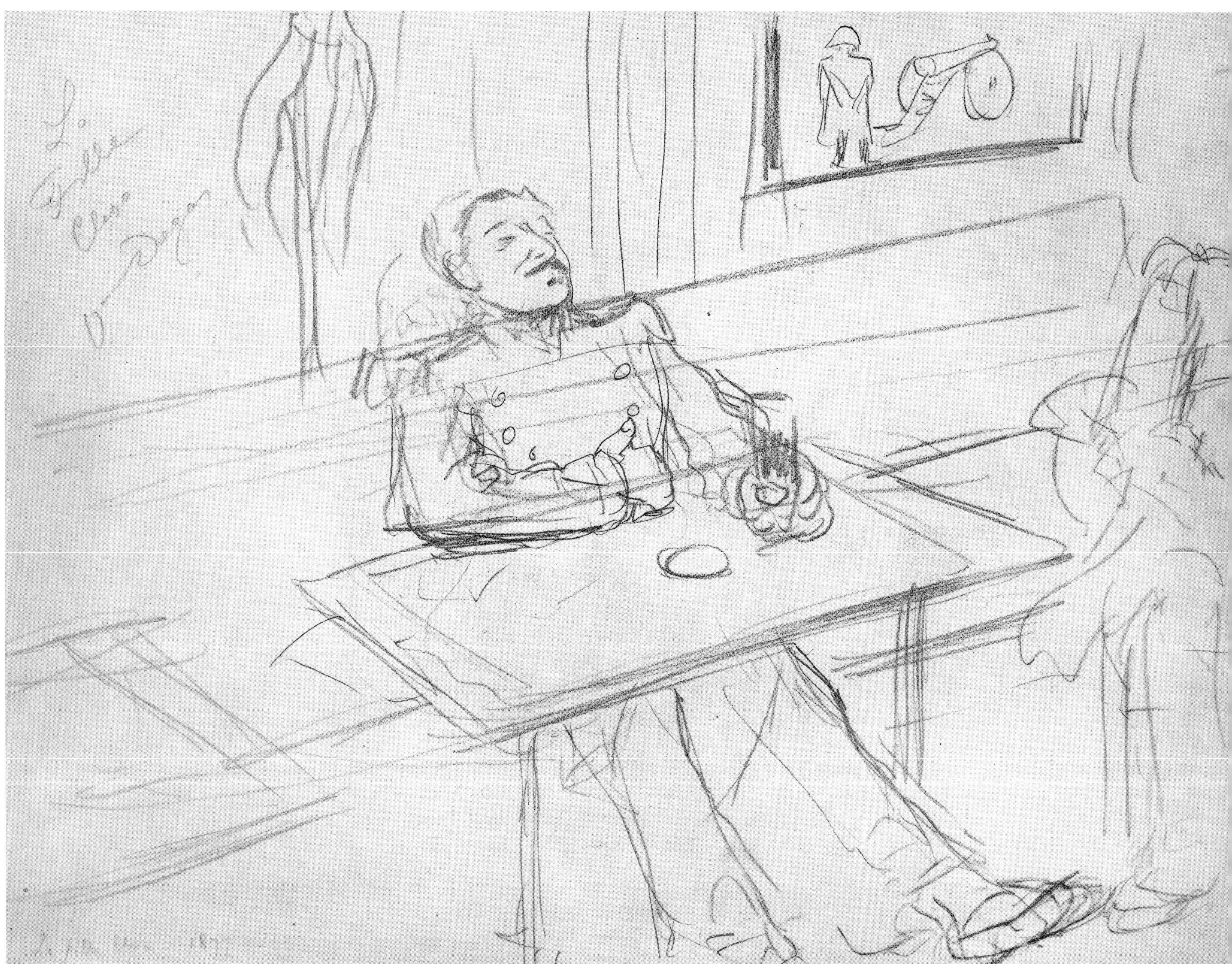
La Fille Elisa
Degas
1877

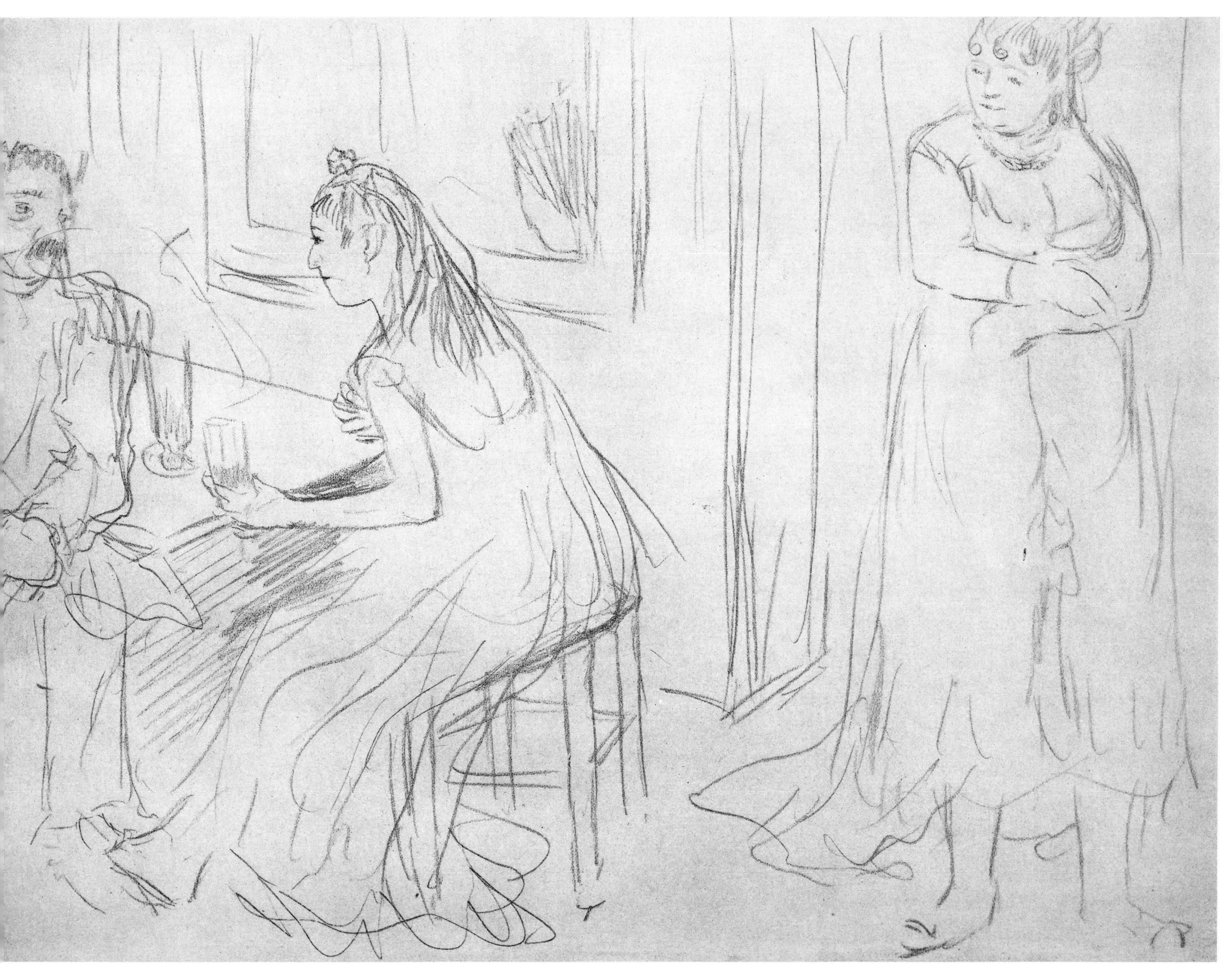

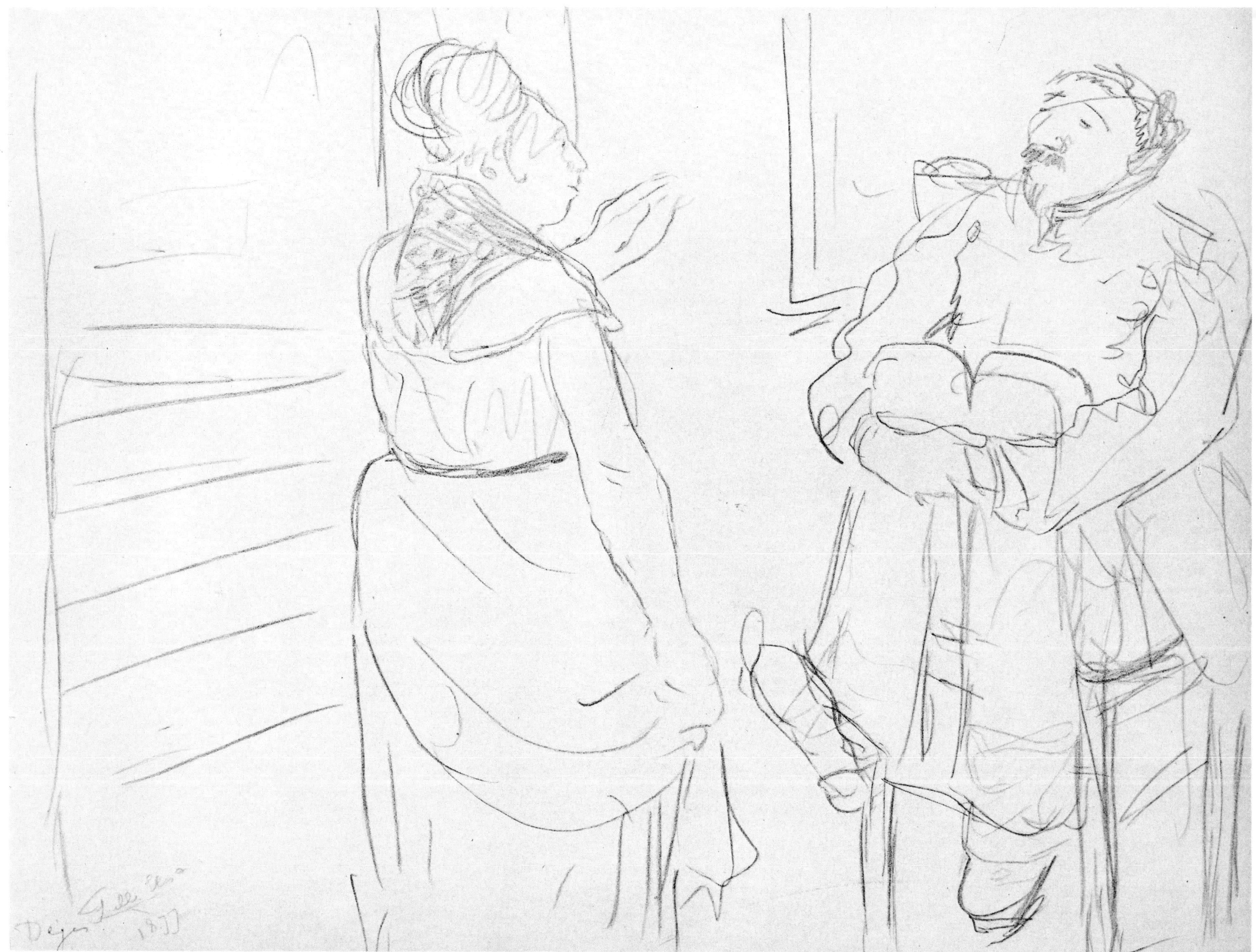
Degas
1877

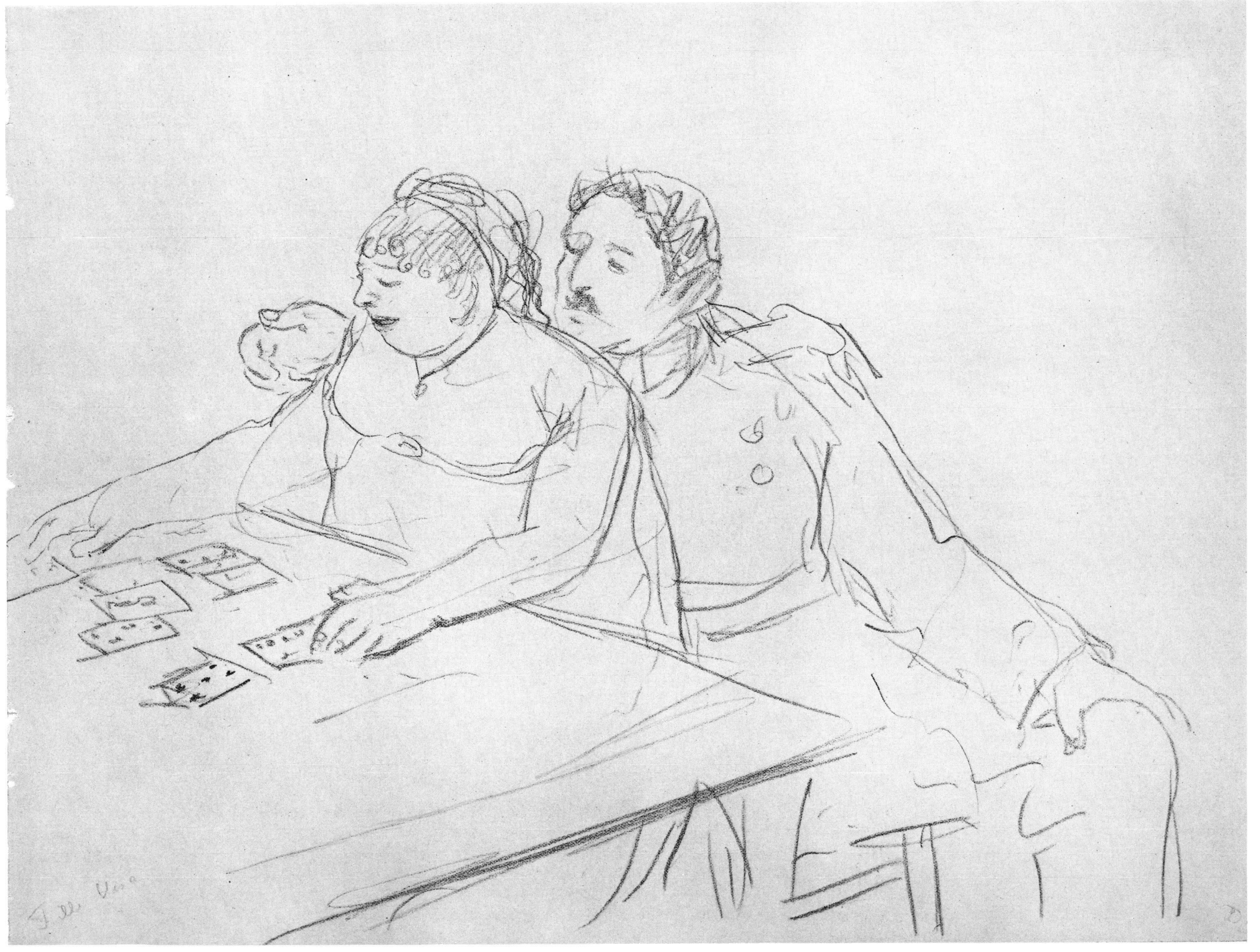

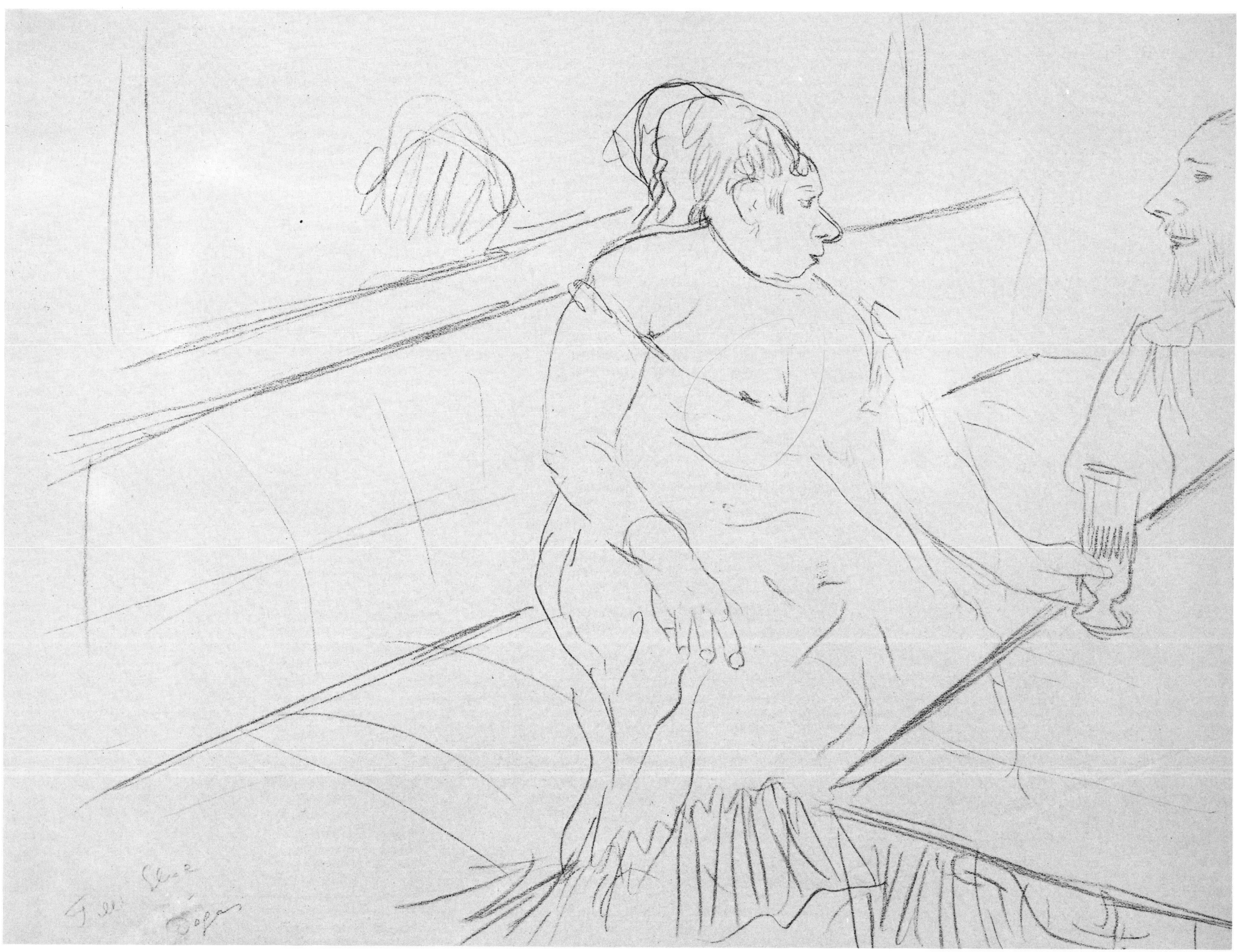

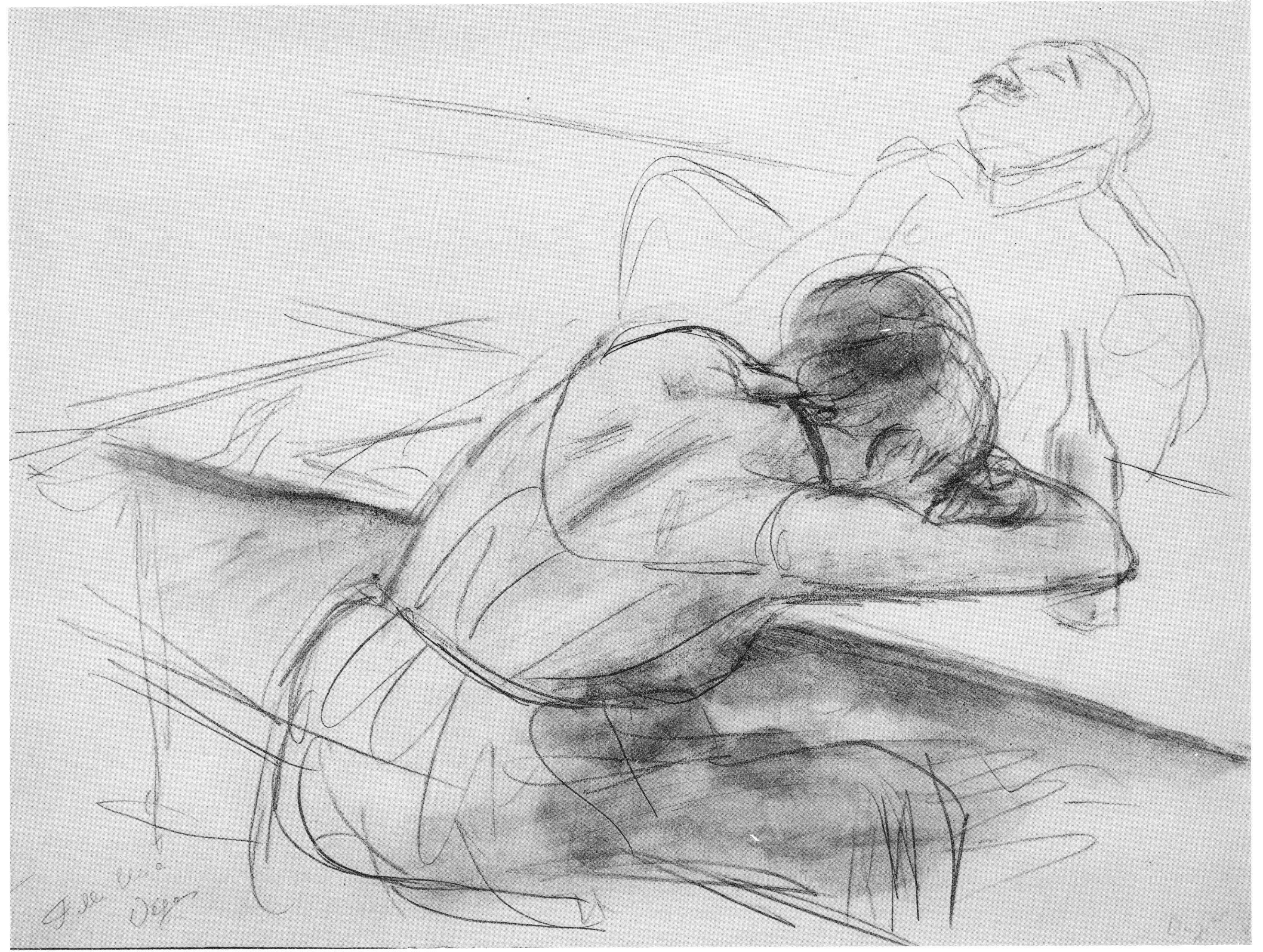

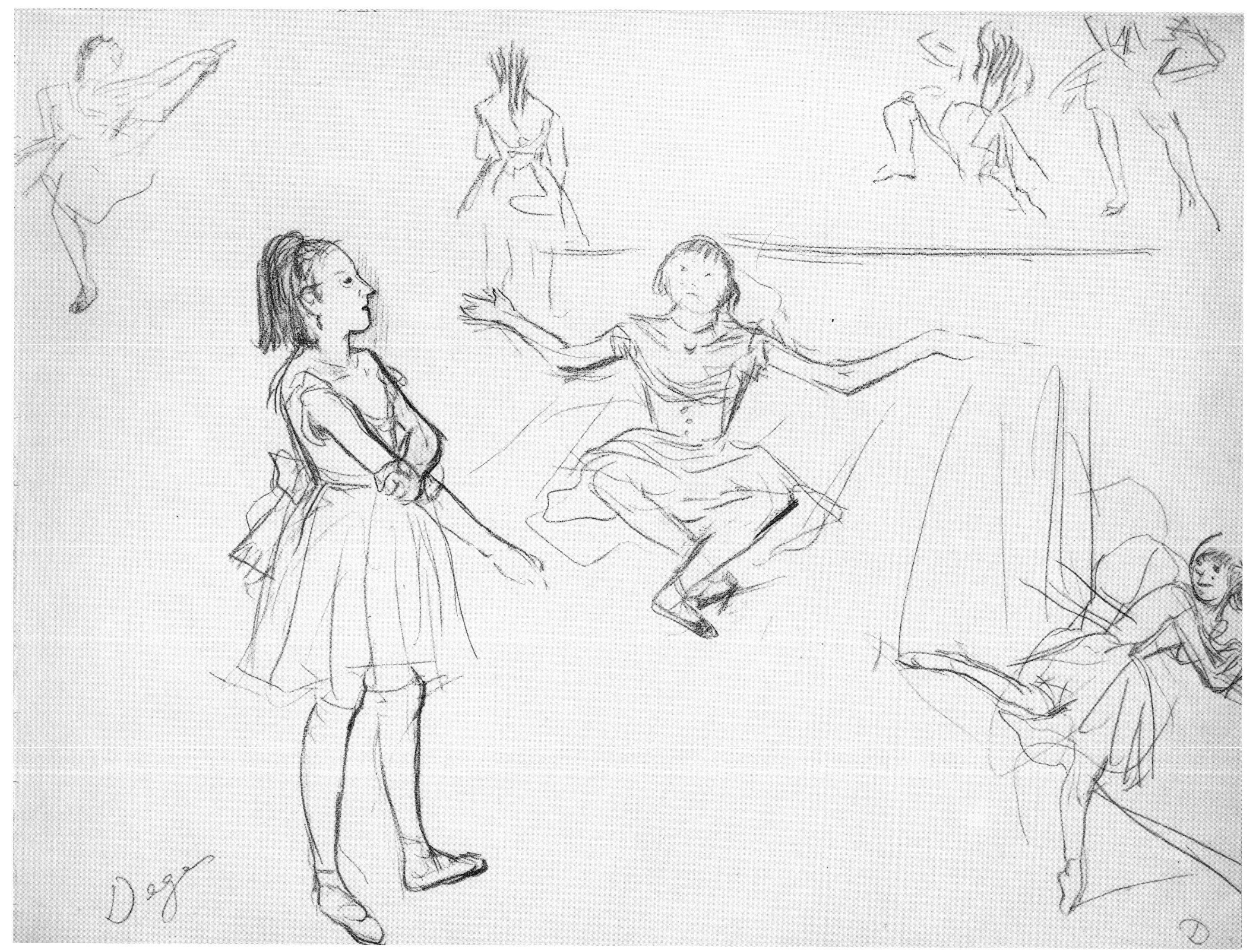

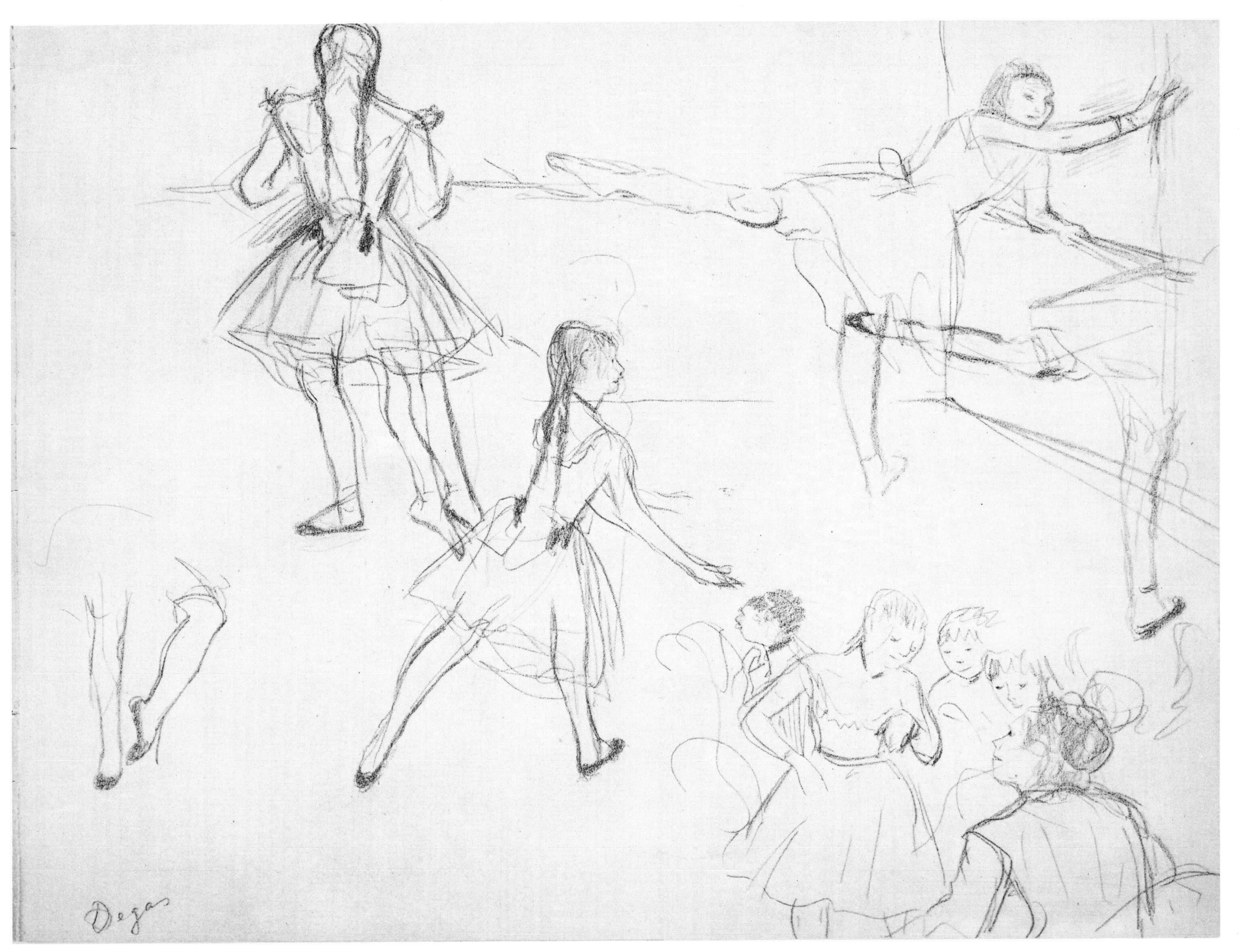
Degas

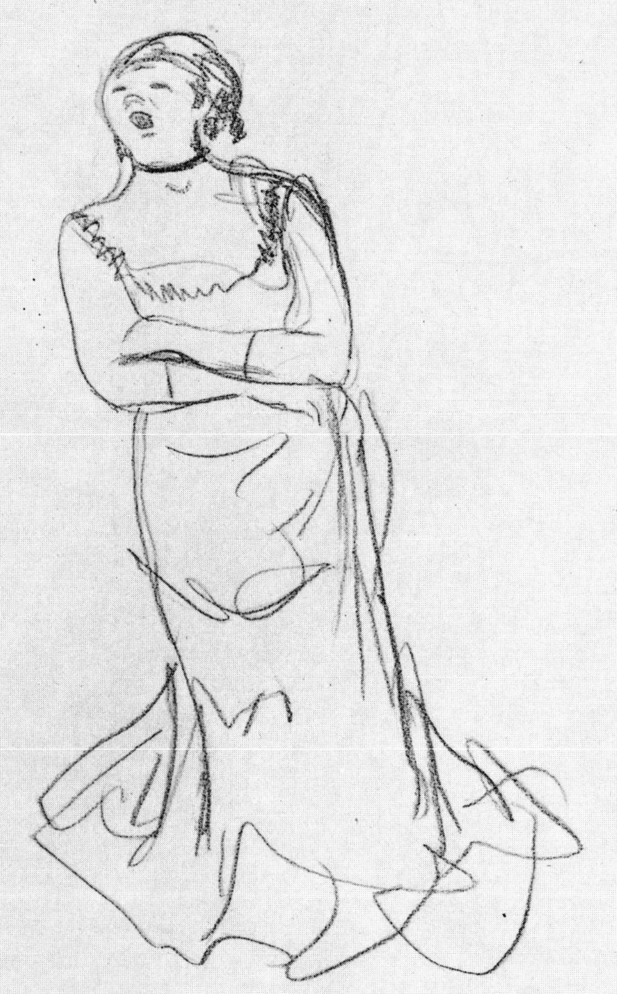

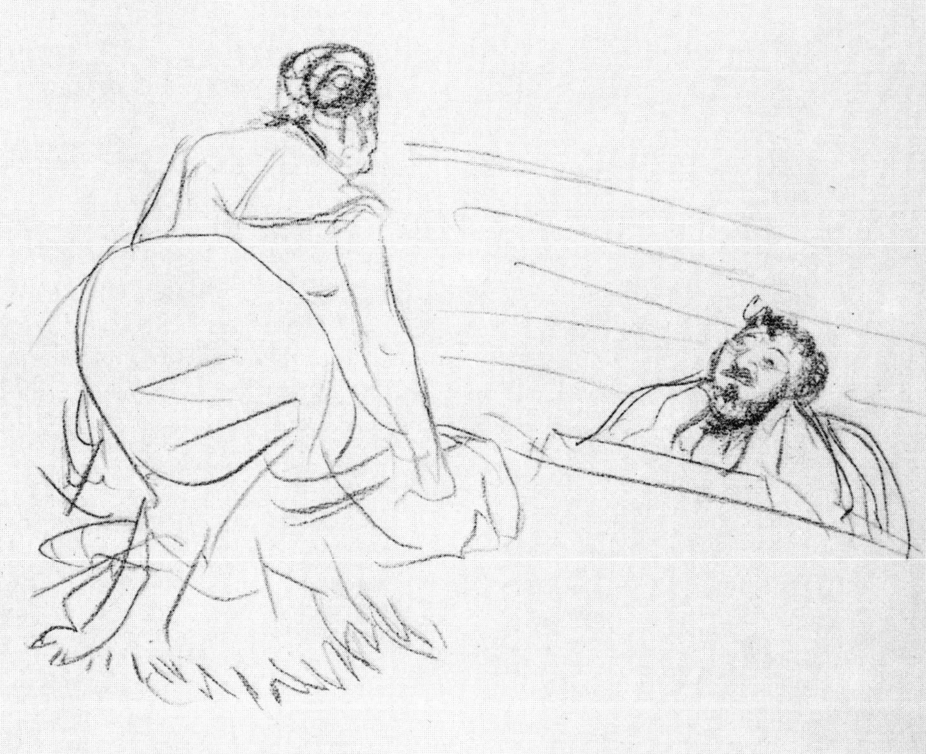
Degas

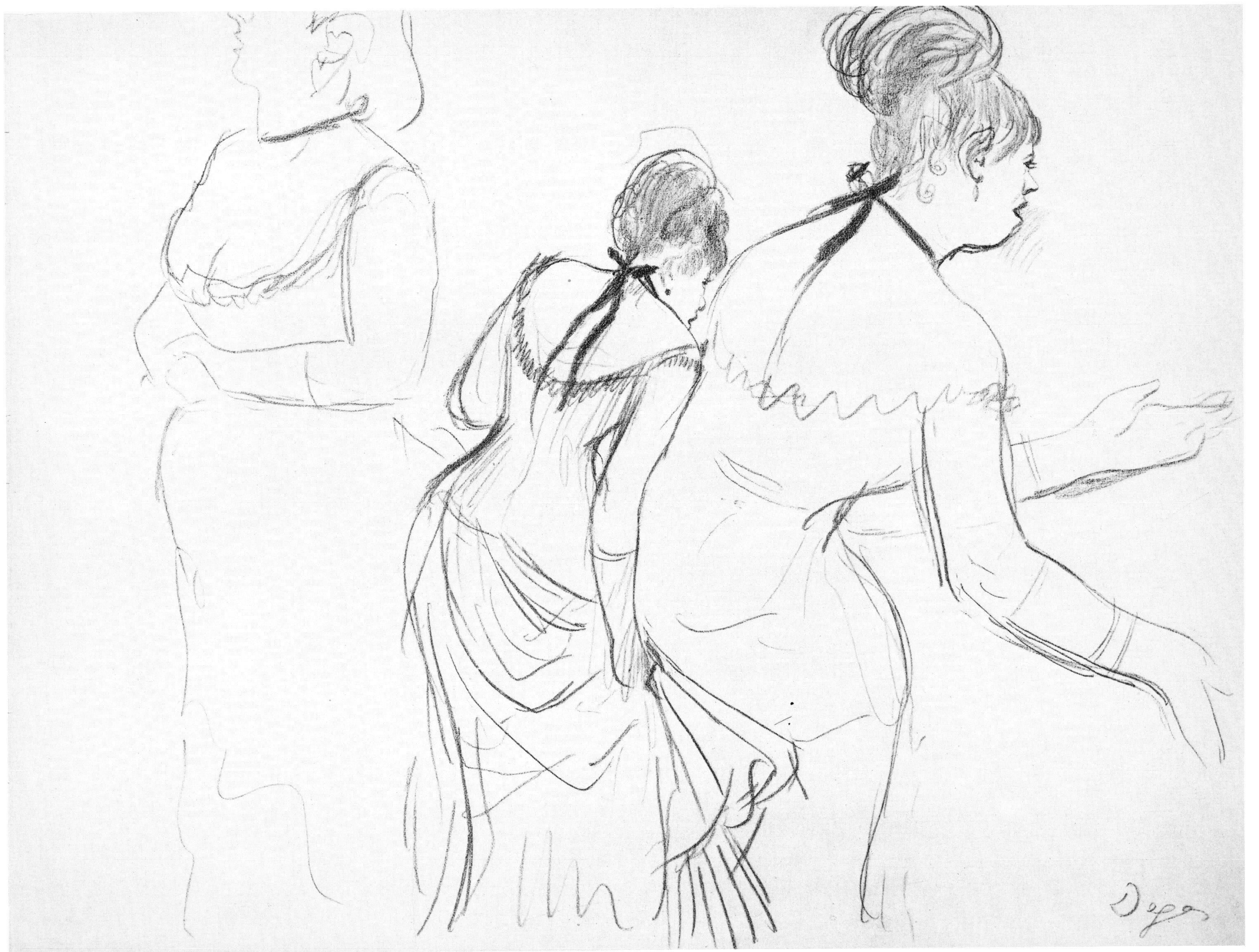
Degas

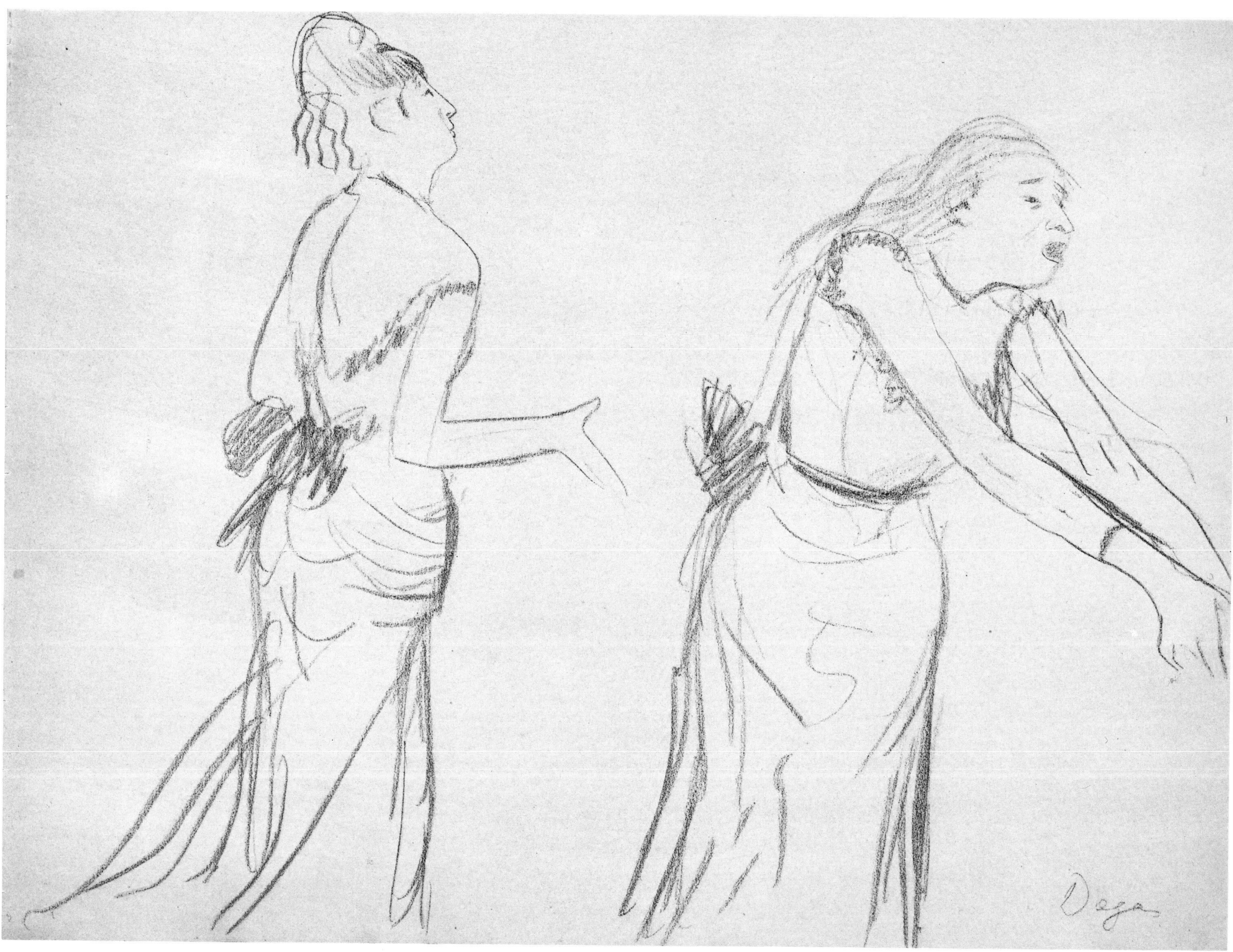
Degas

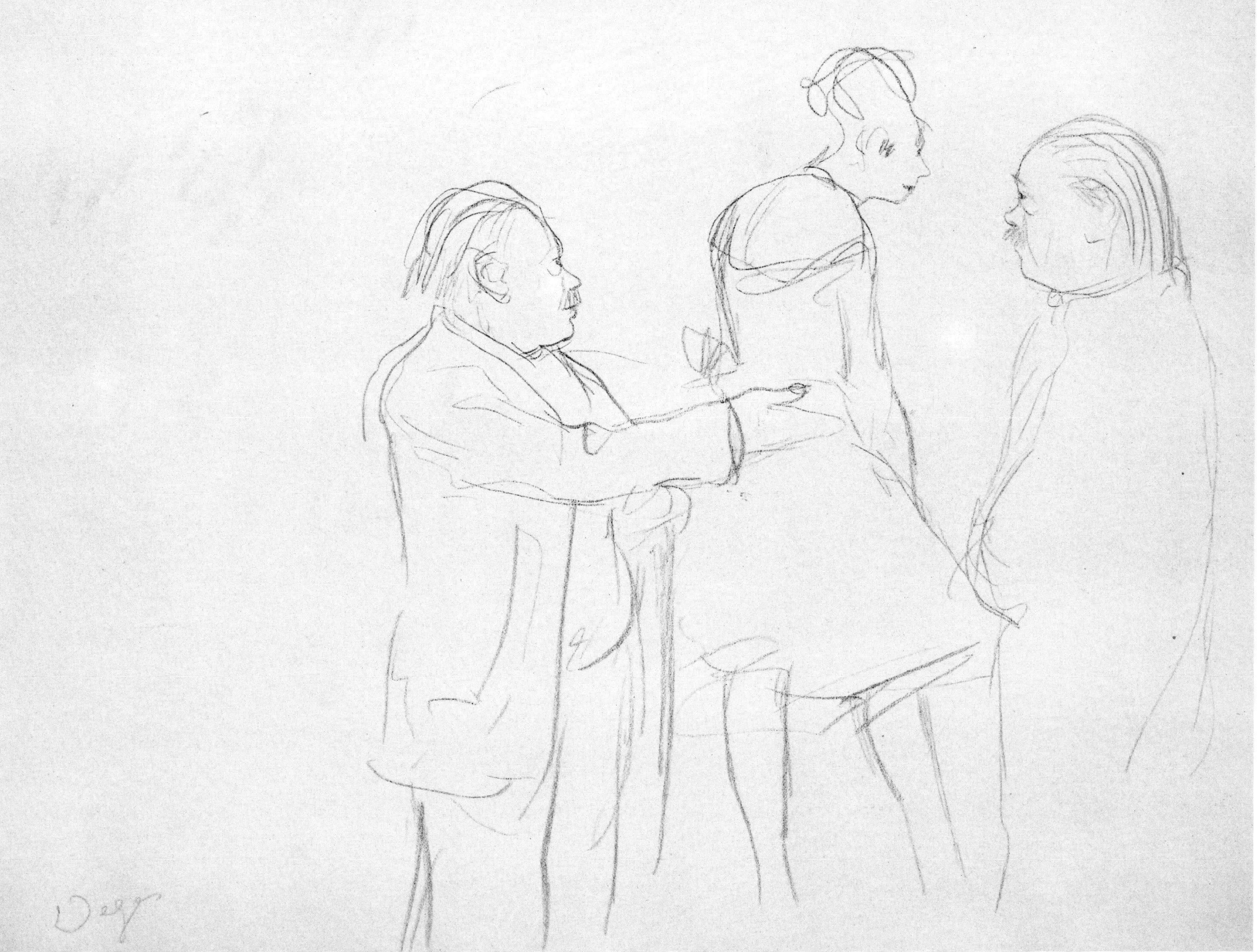

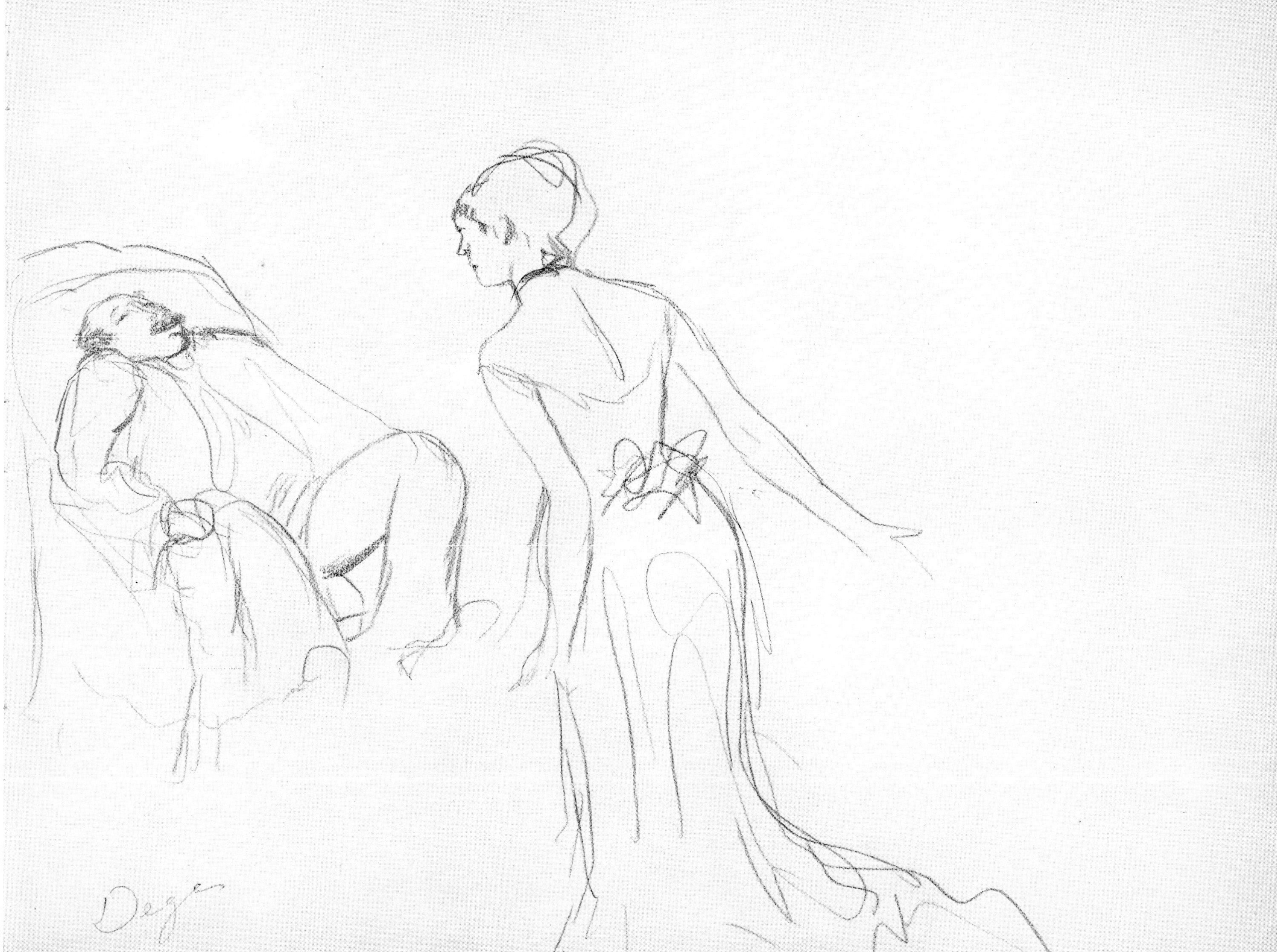

Degas

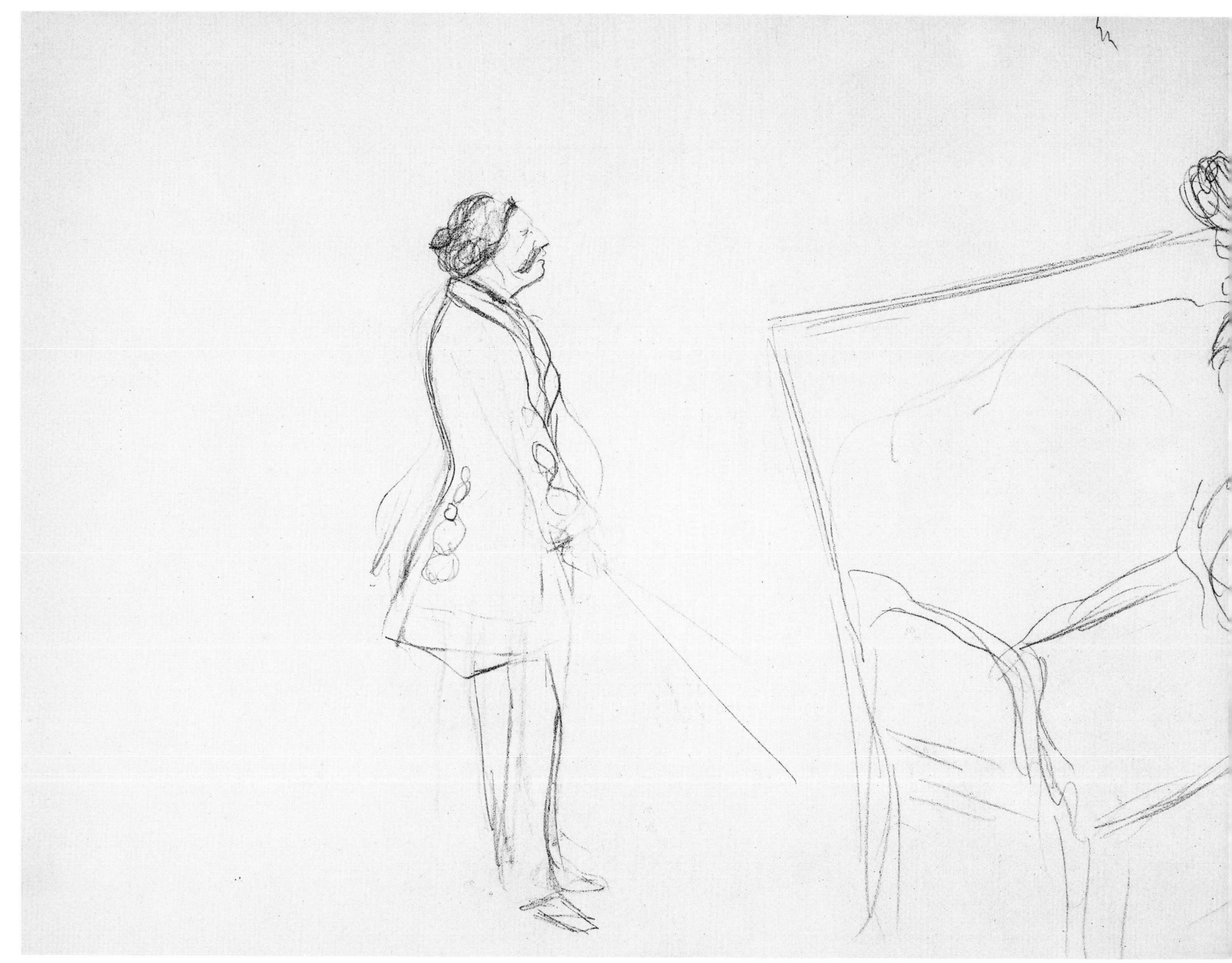

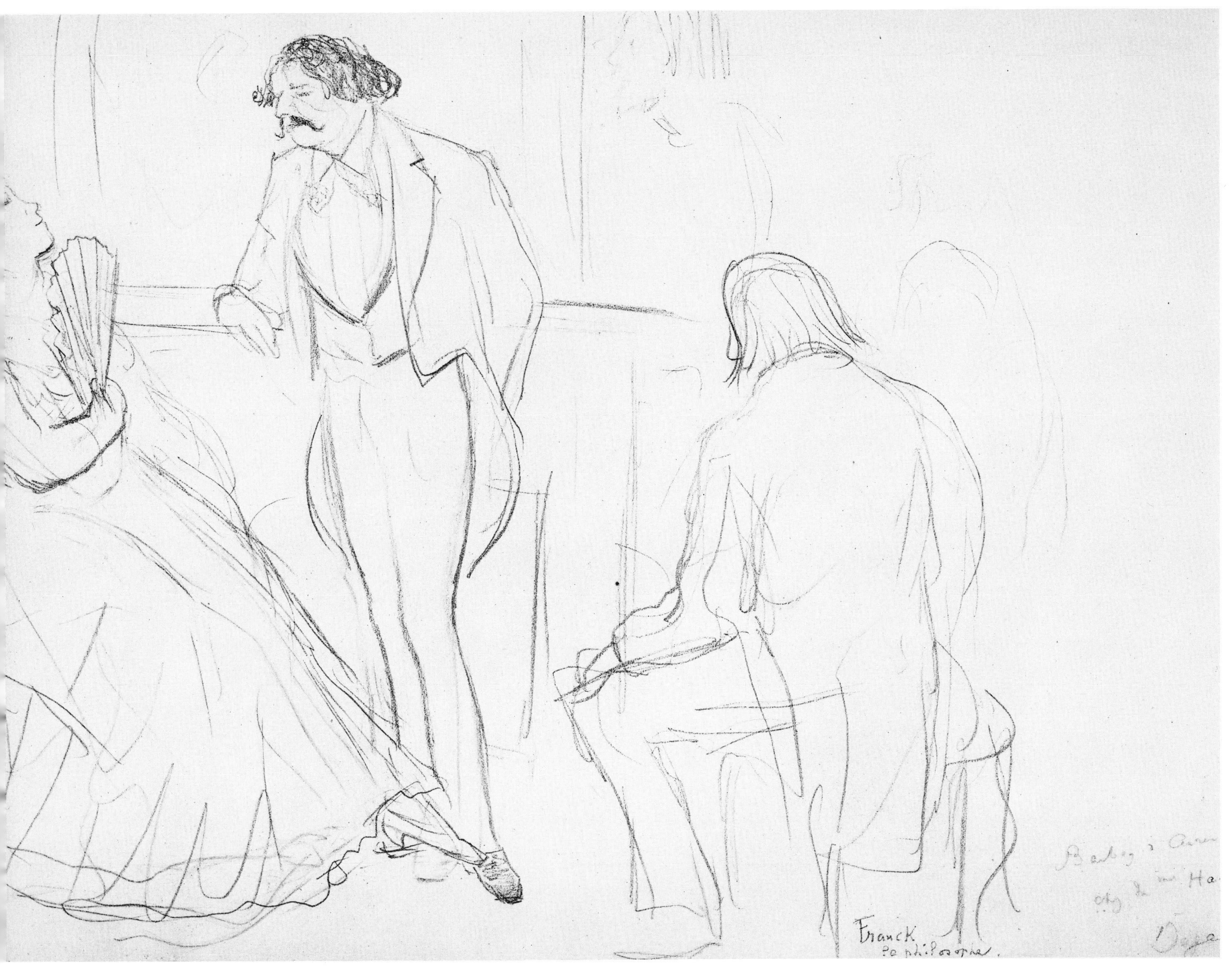
Franck
le philosophe.

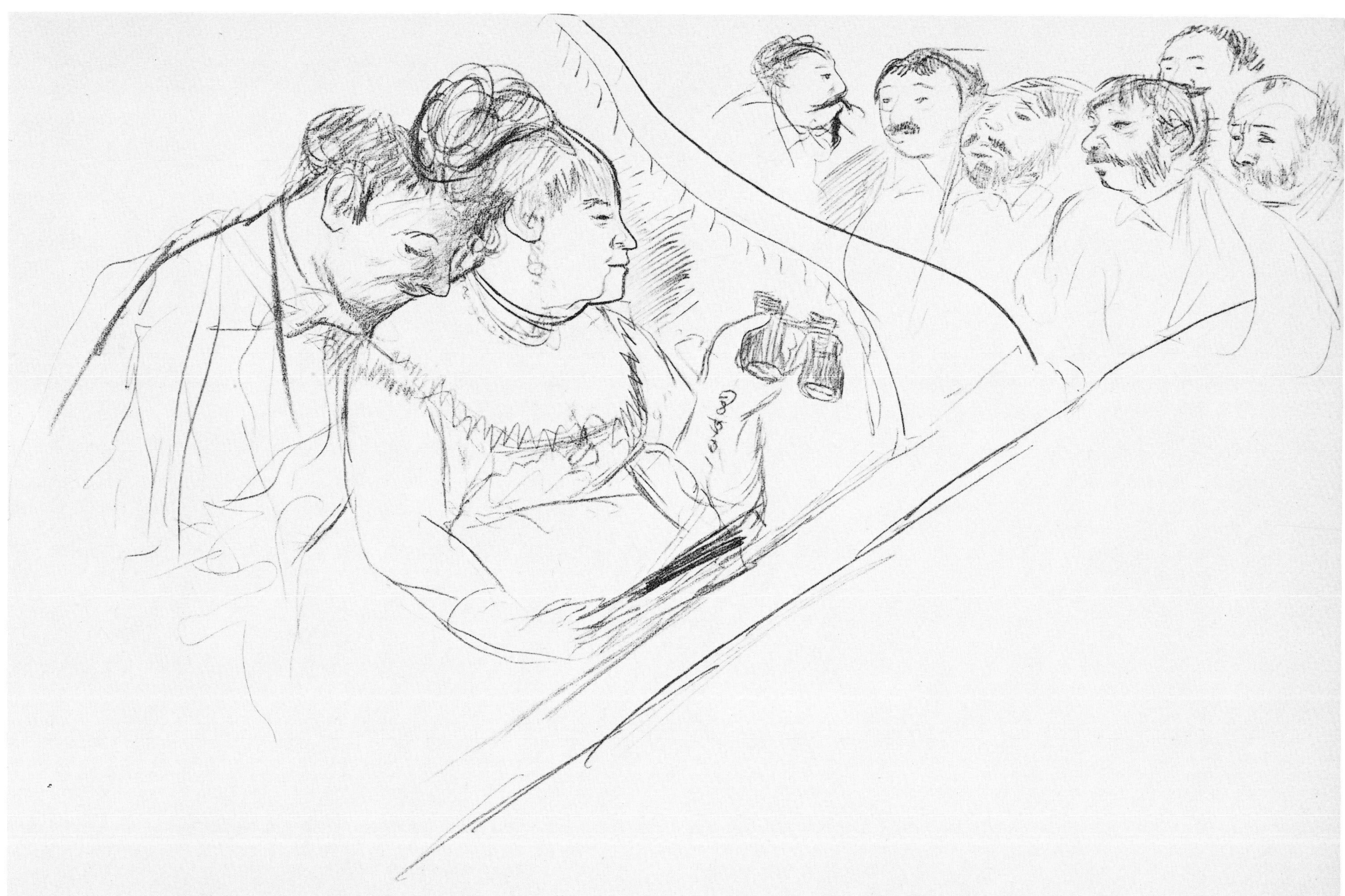

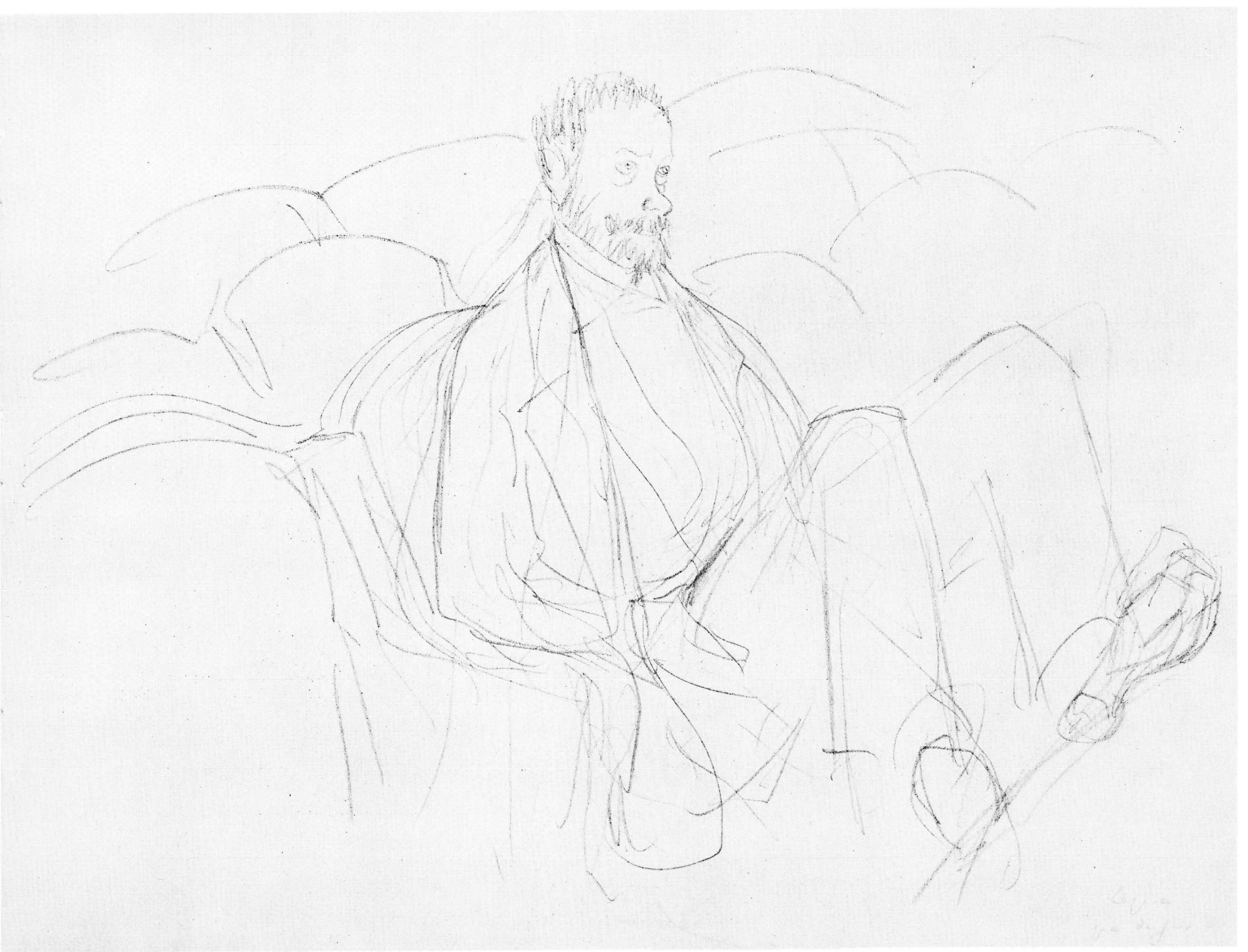

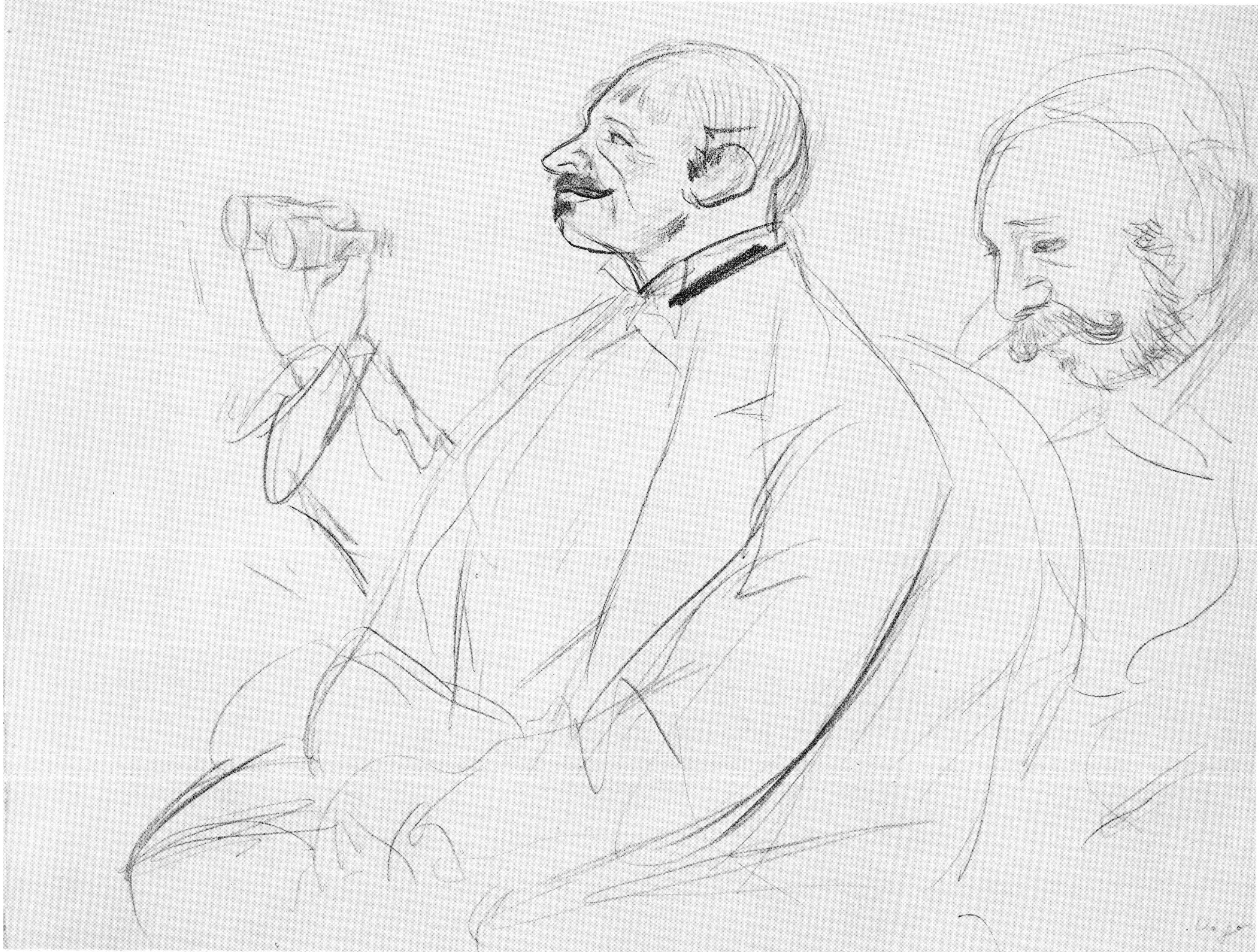
Degas

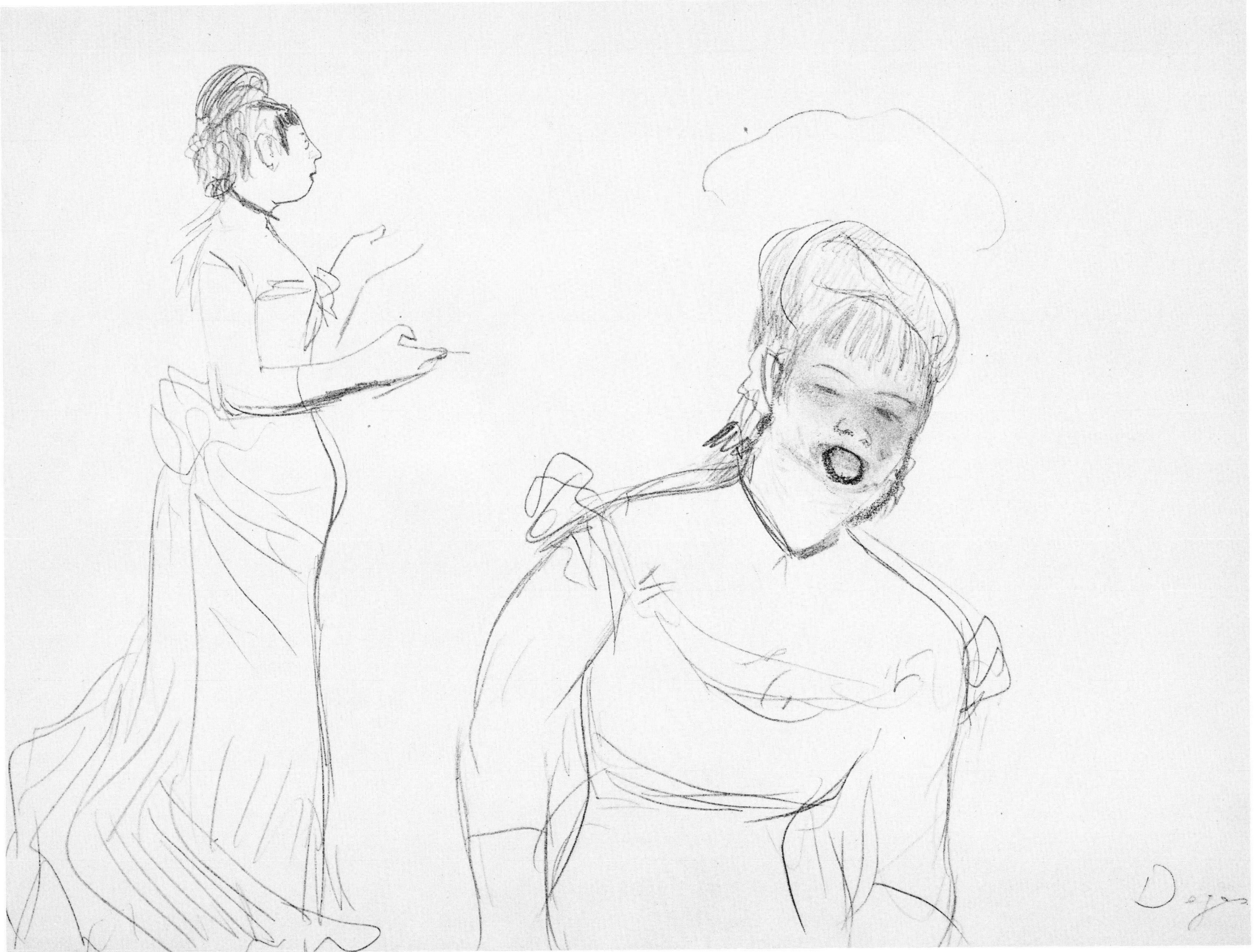

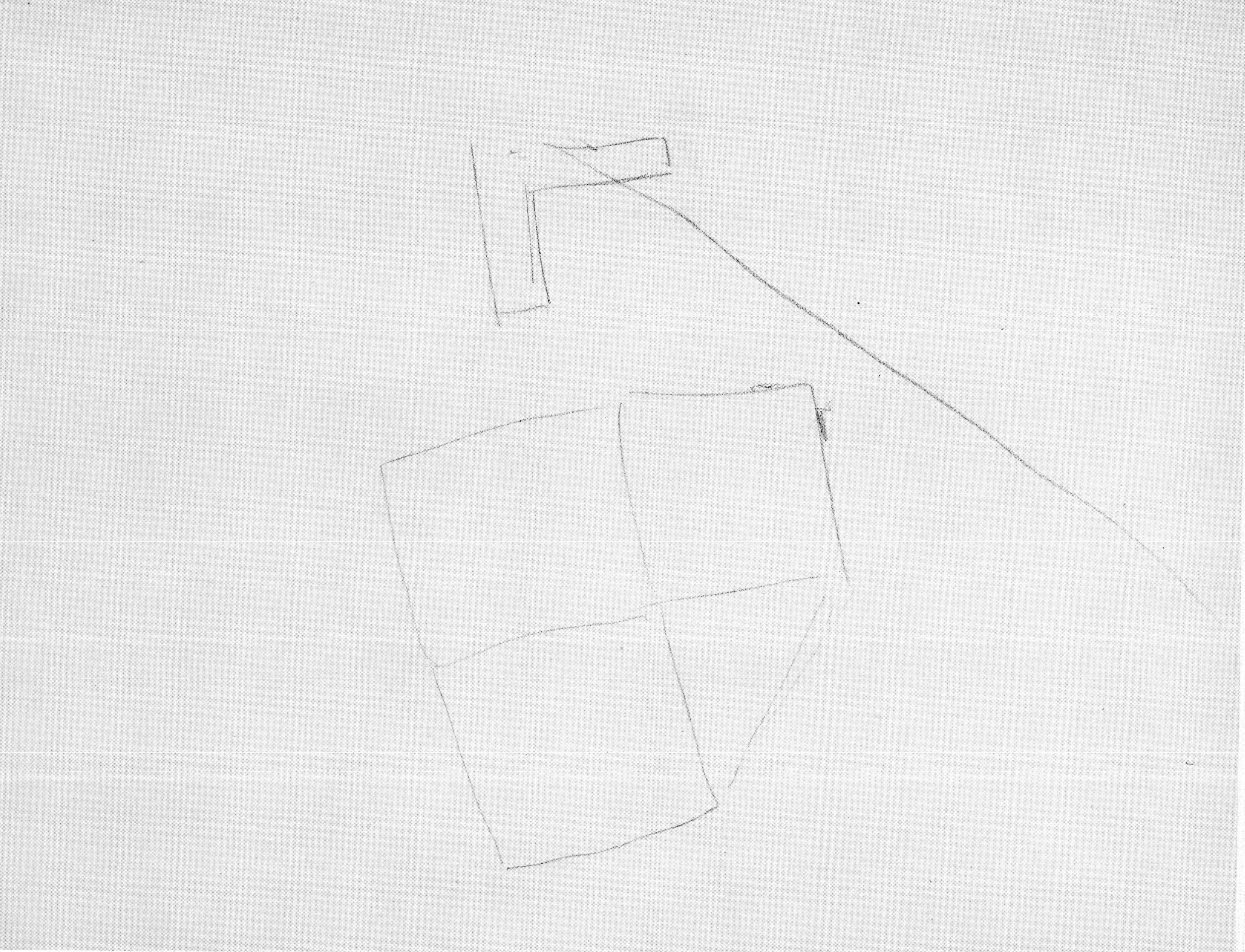

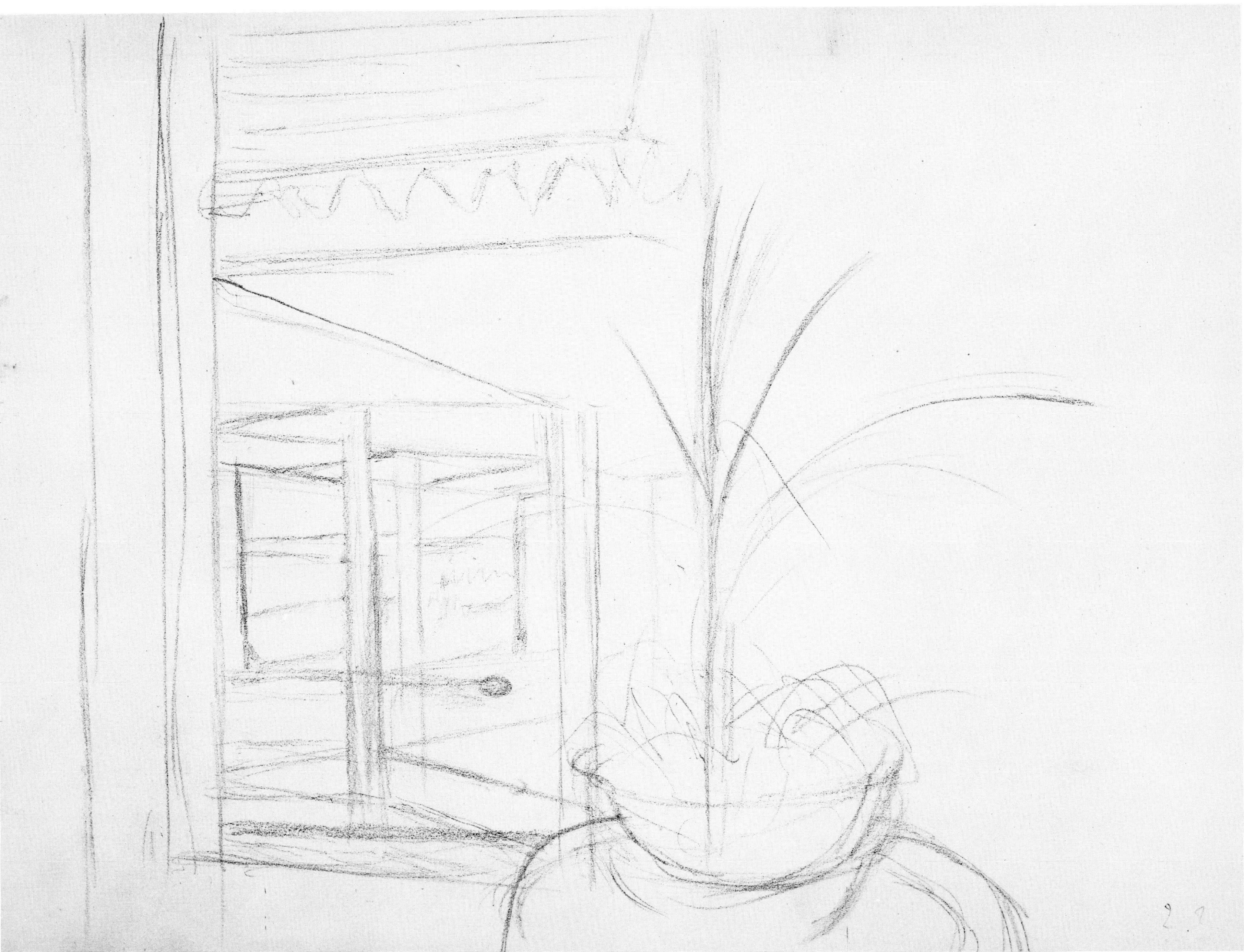

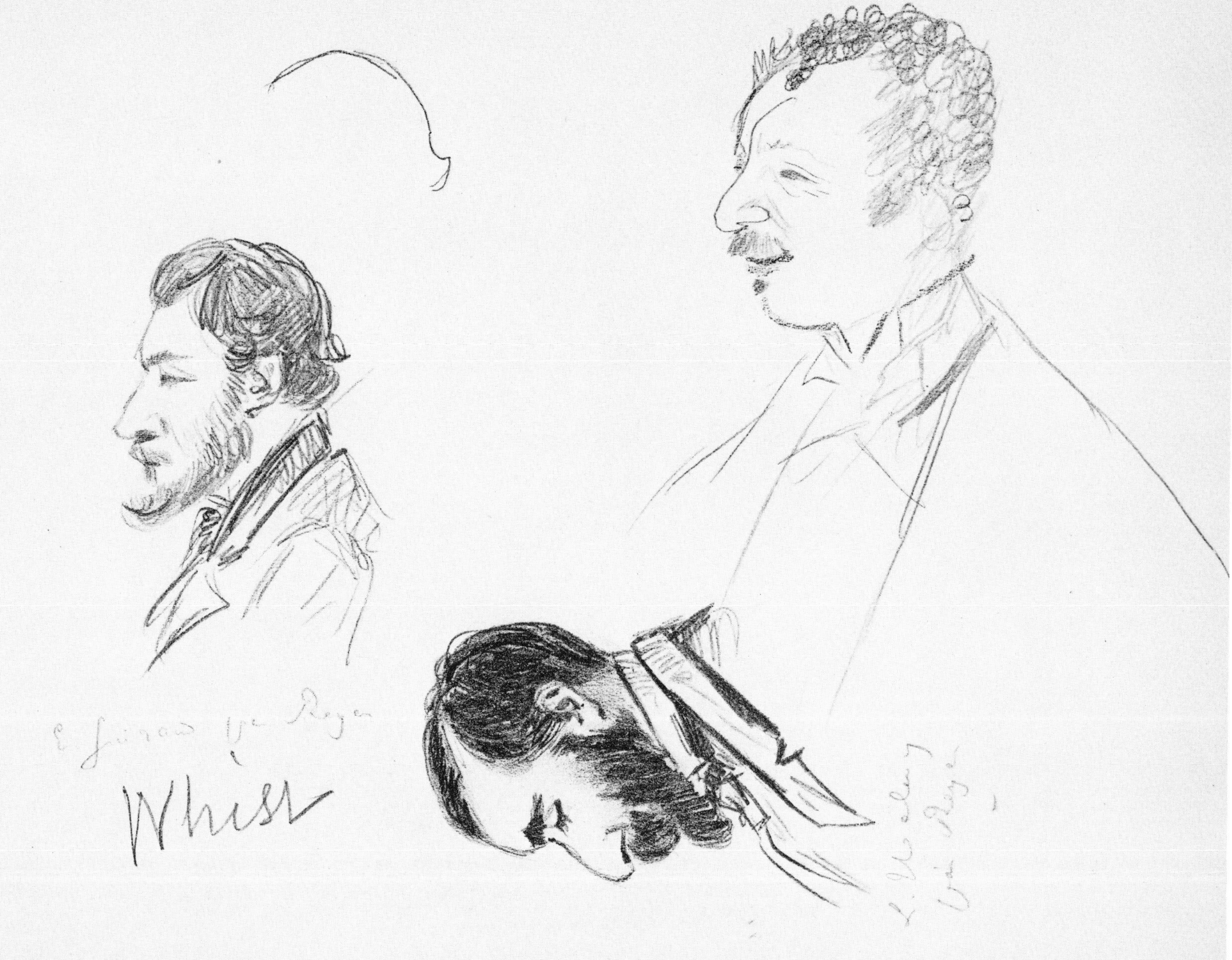
Whist

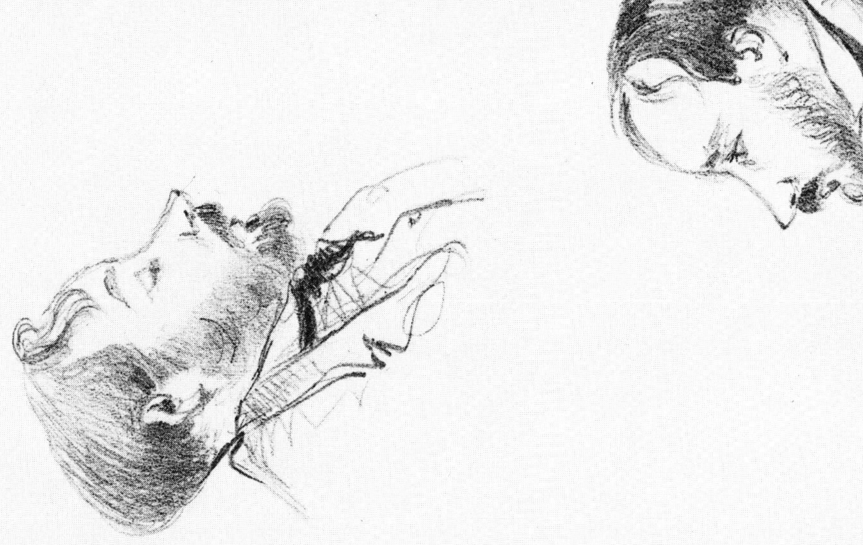

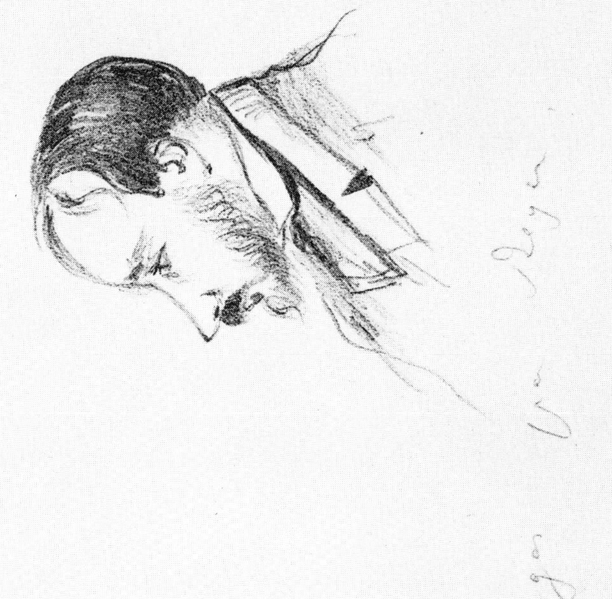

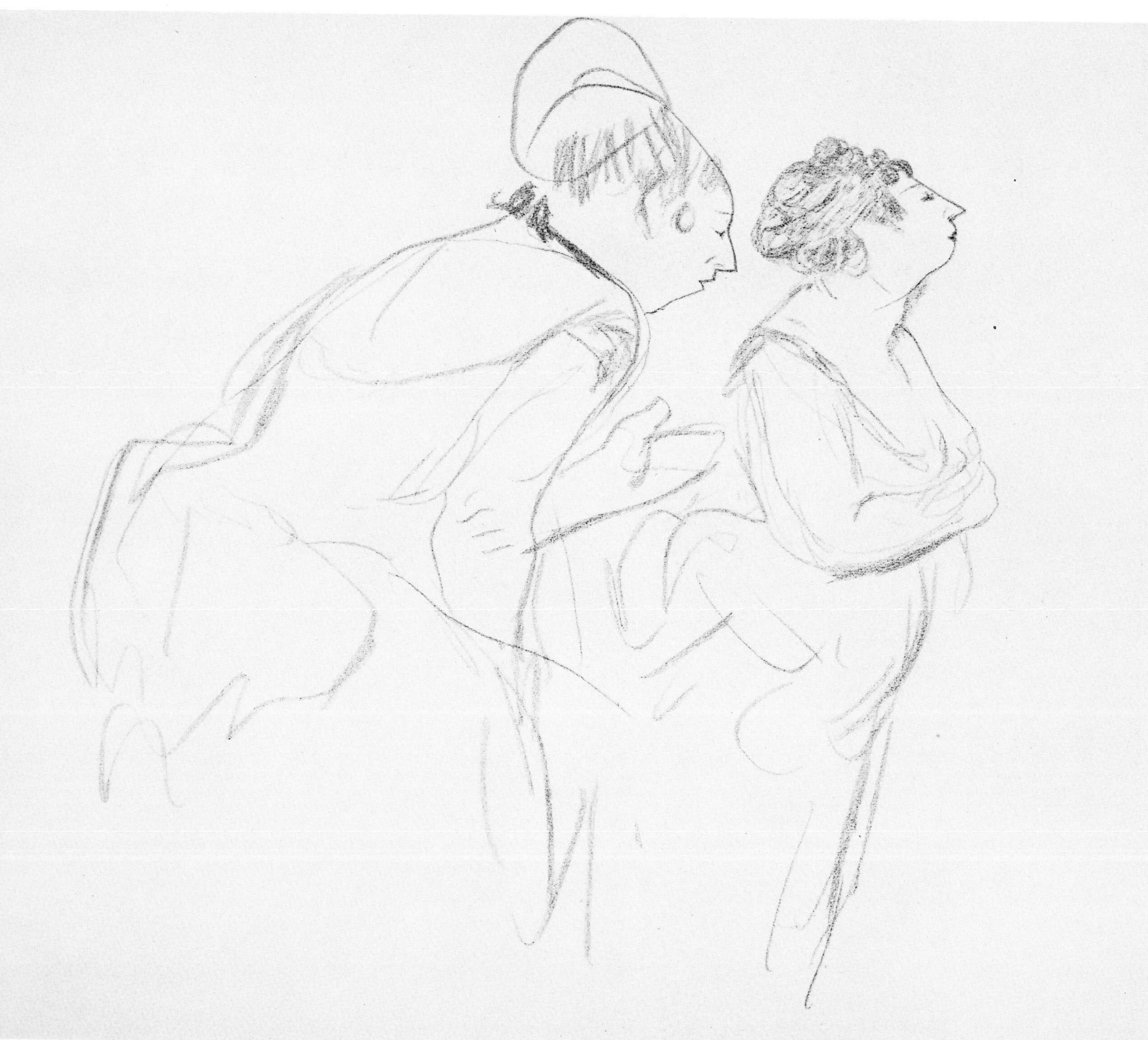

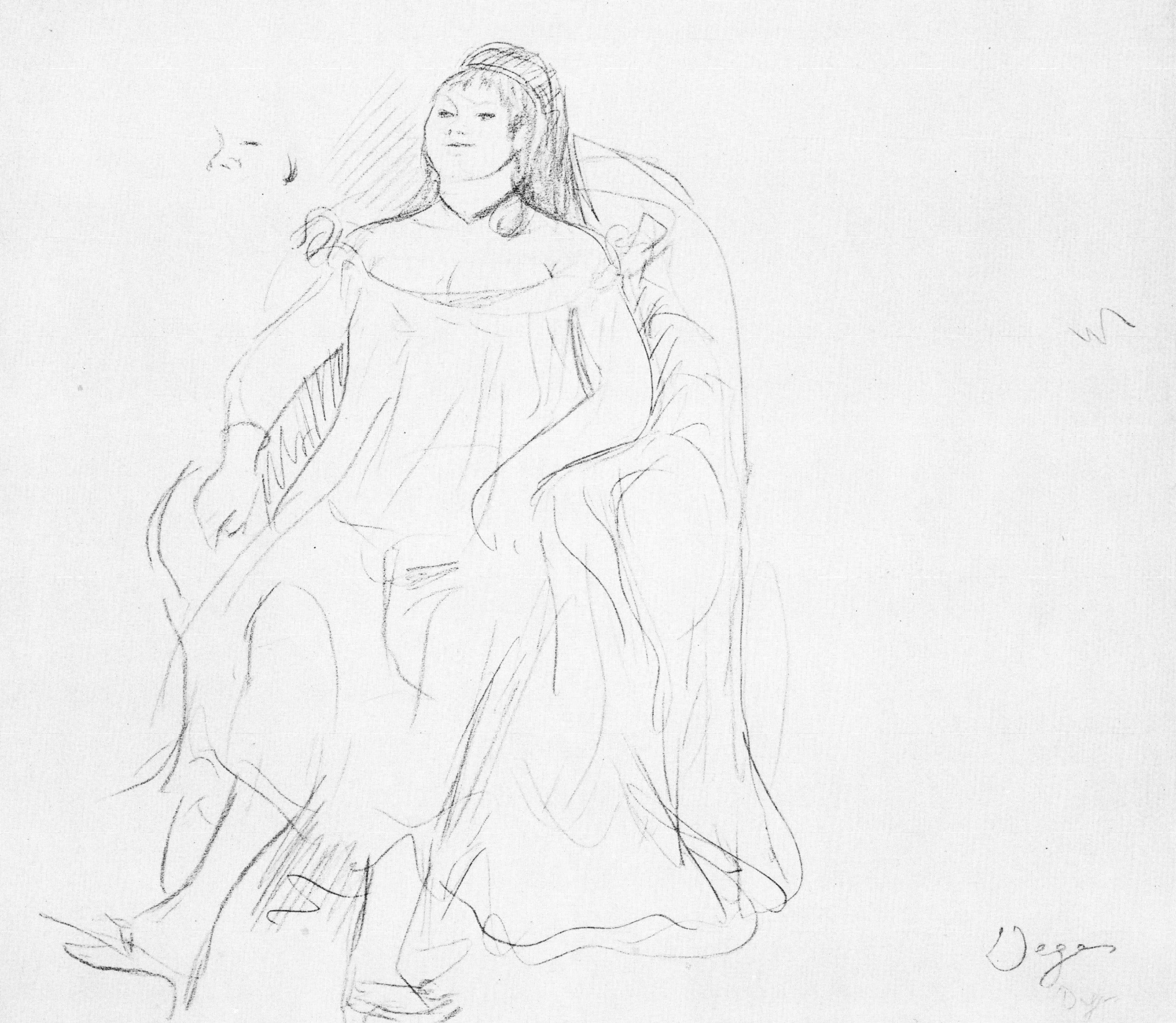
Degas

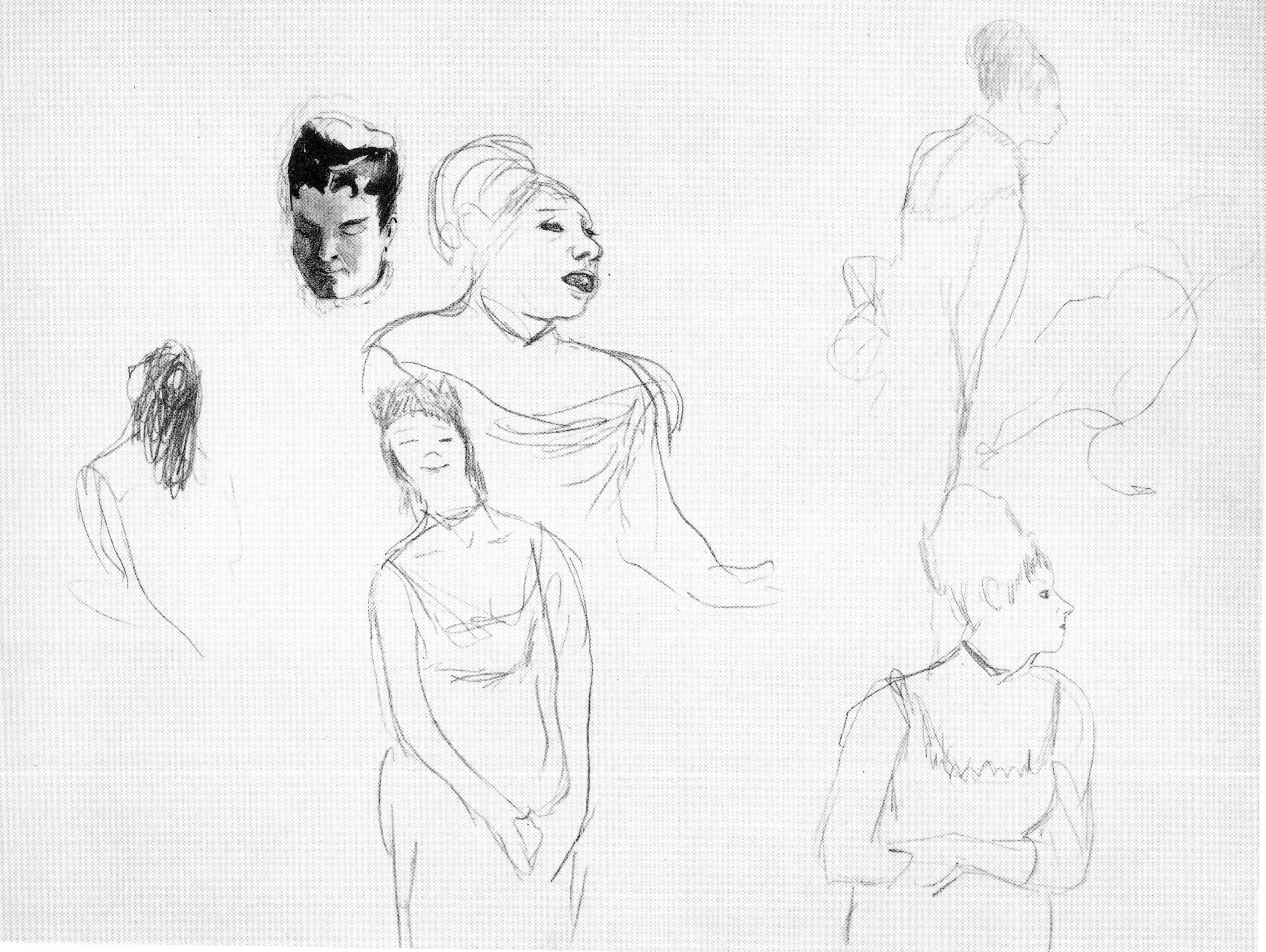

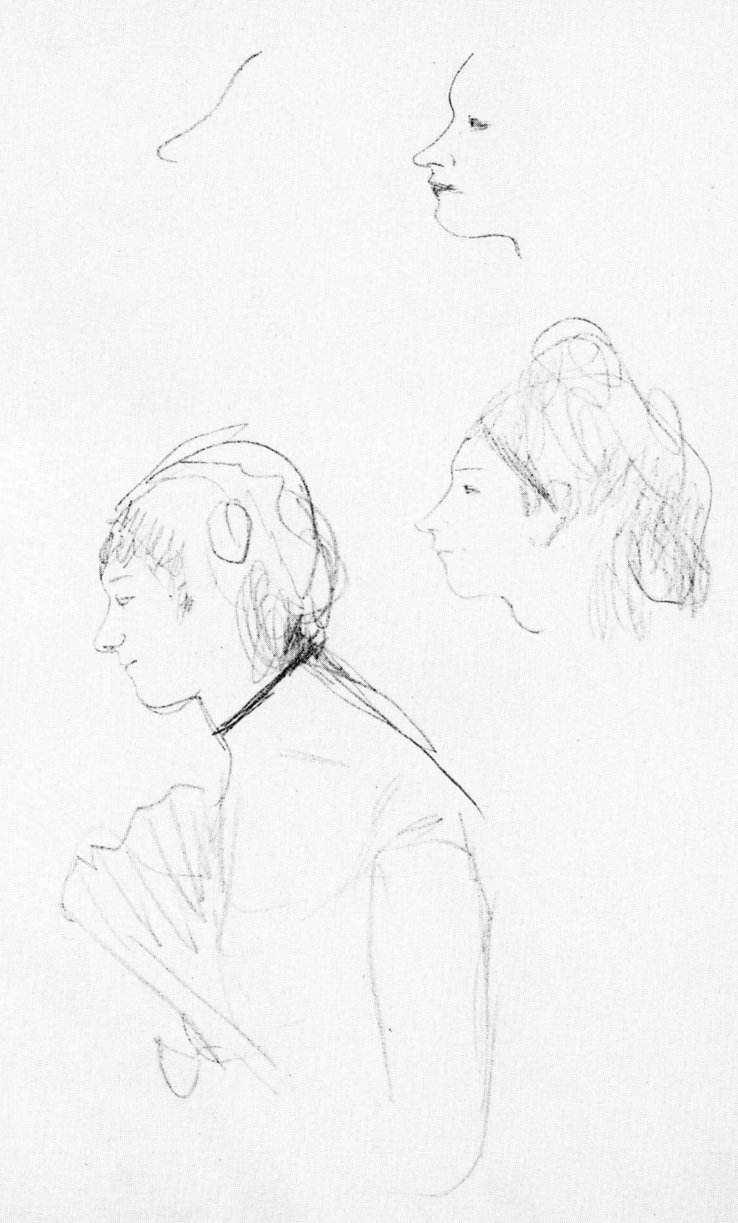

Tous les croquis de cet album
ont été faits chez moi par Degas

Années 1880 et suivantes

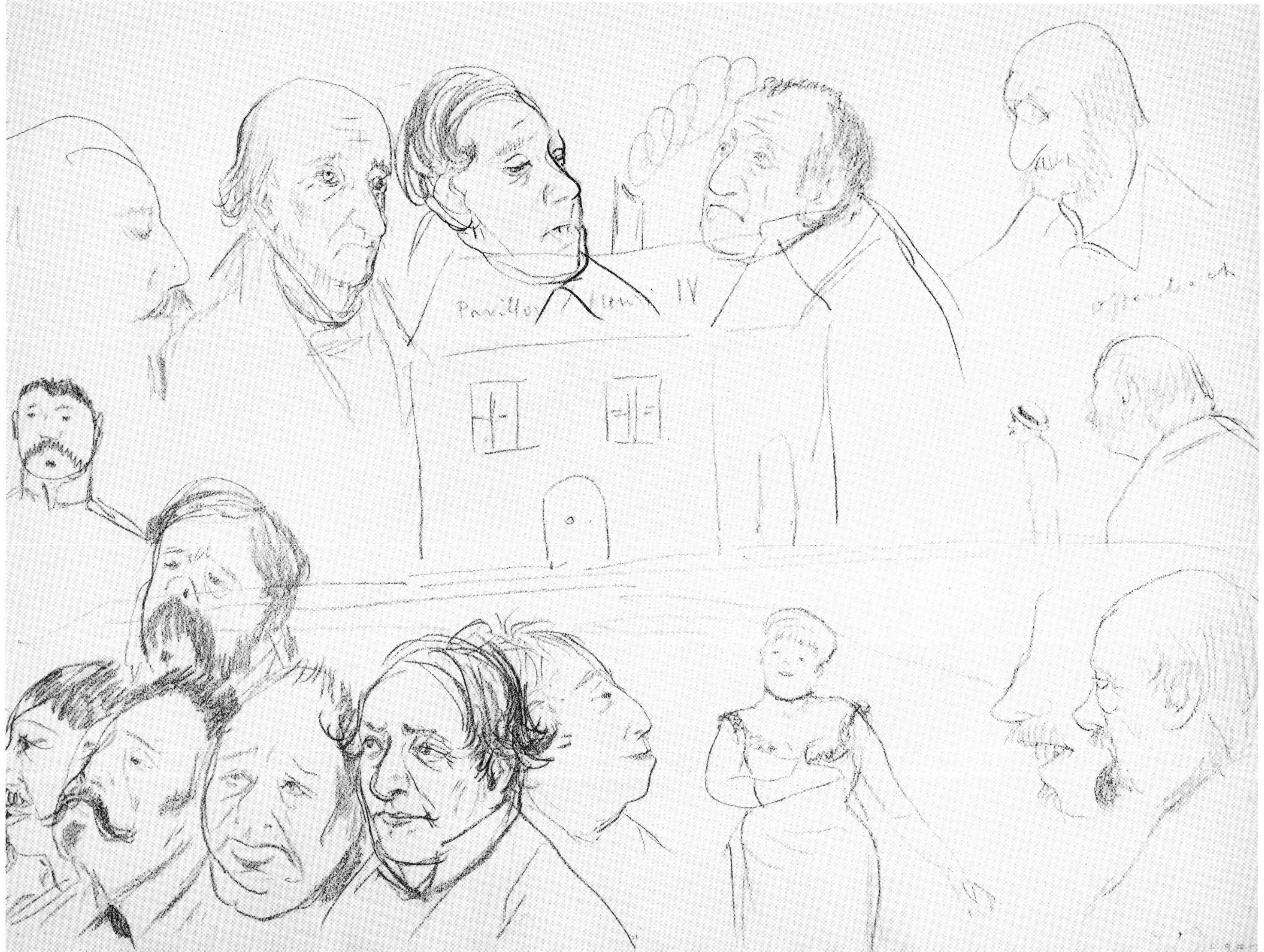

Henri IV
Offenbach

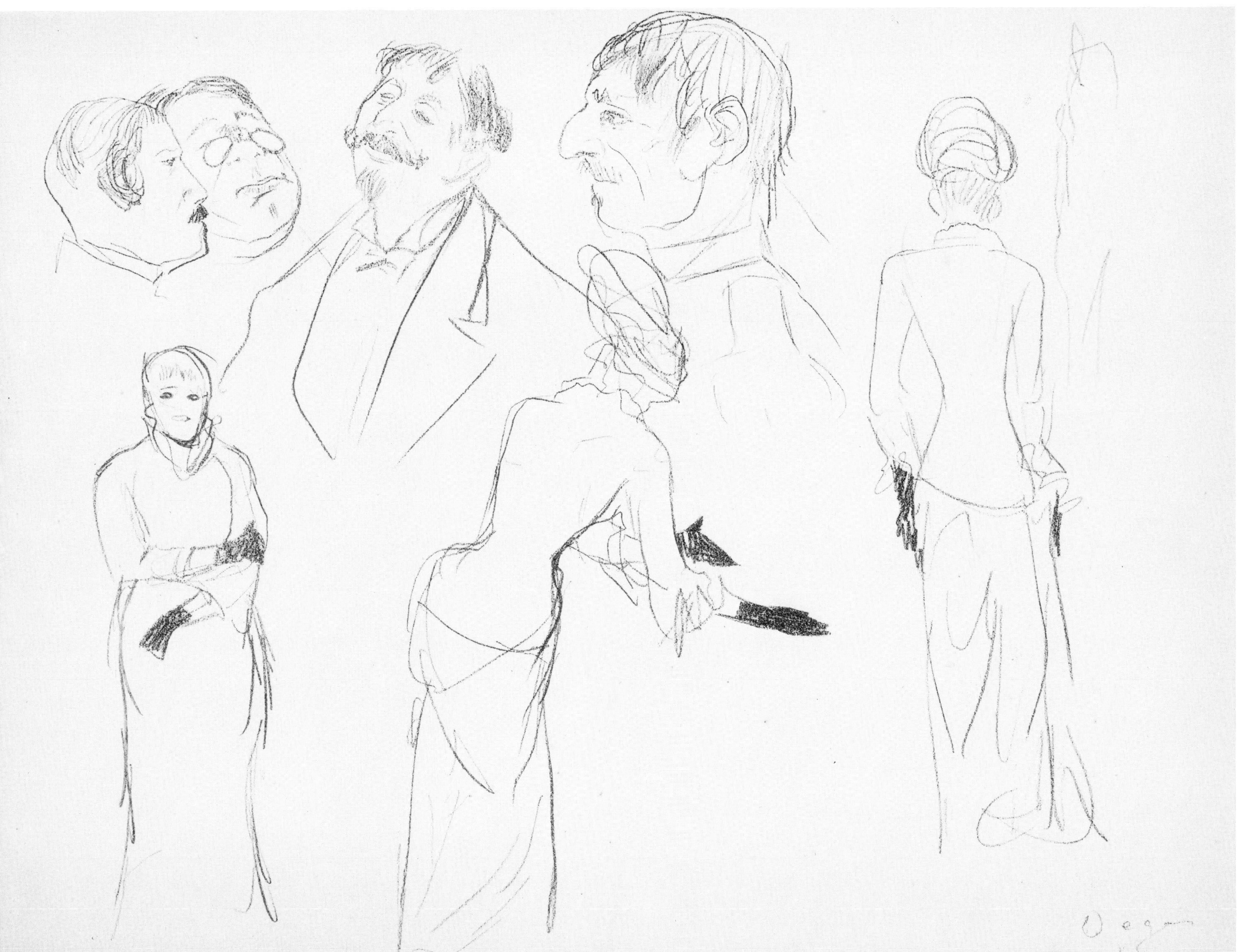
Degas

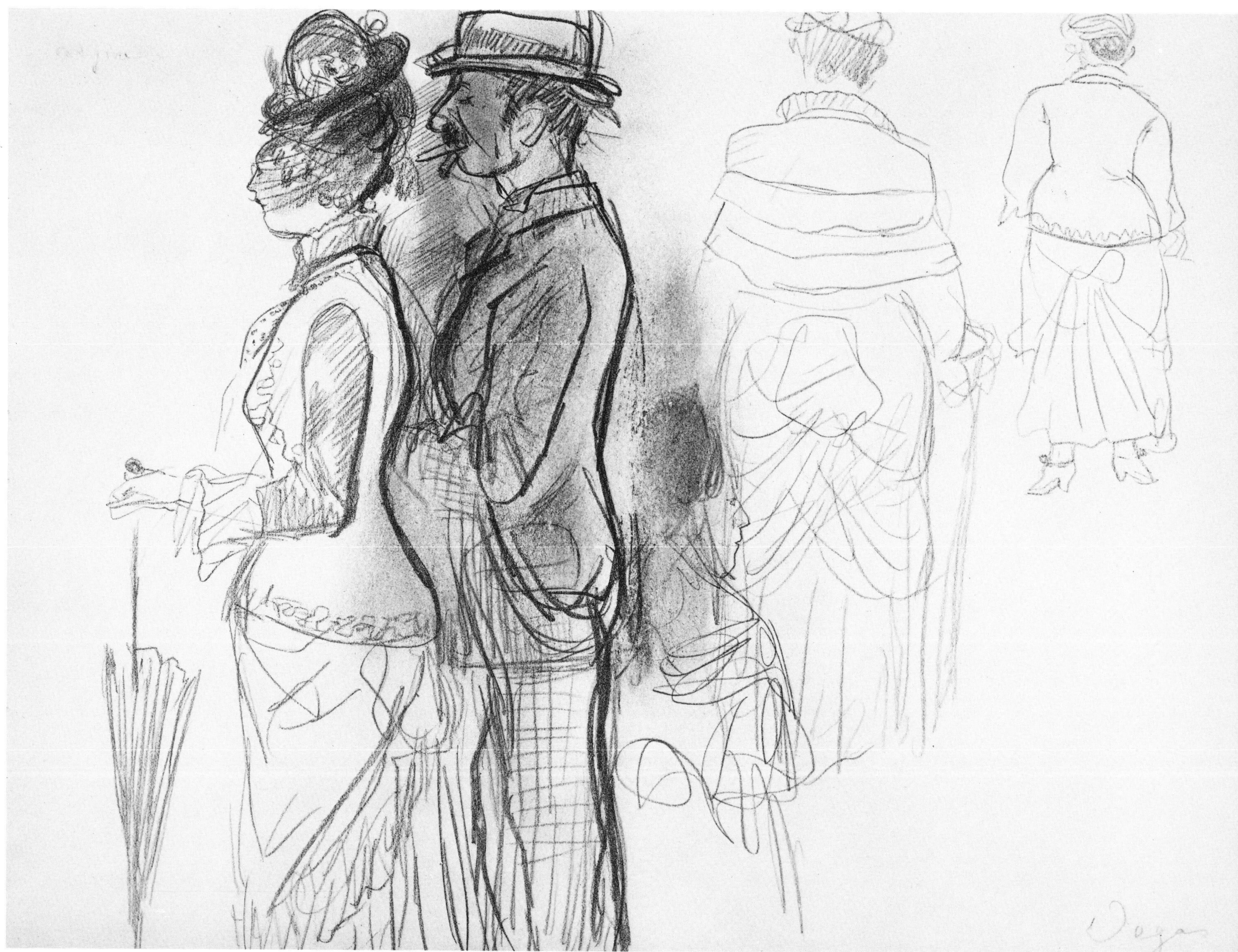

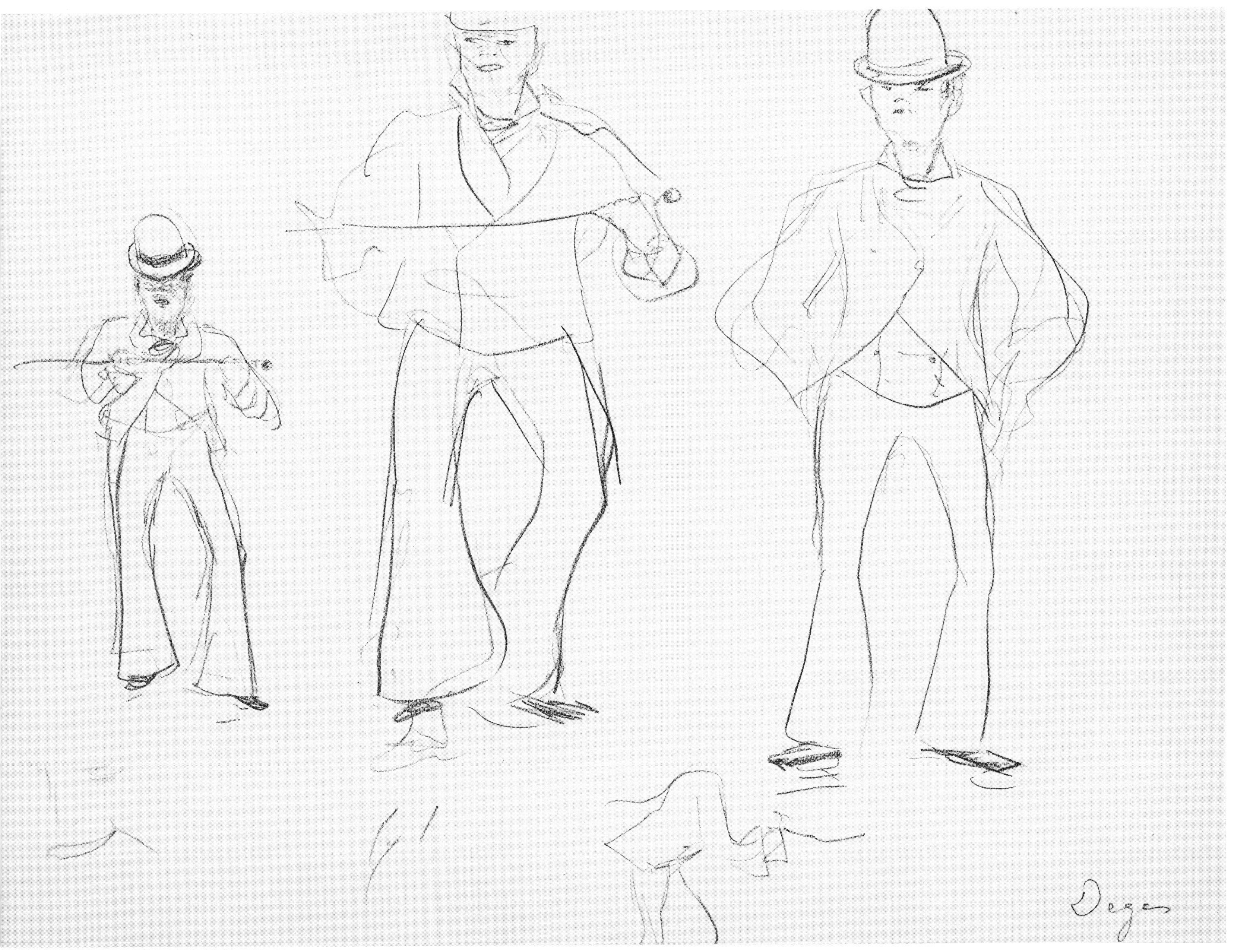
Degas

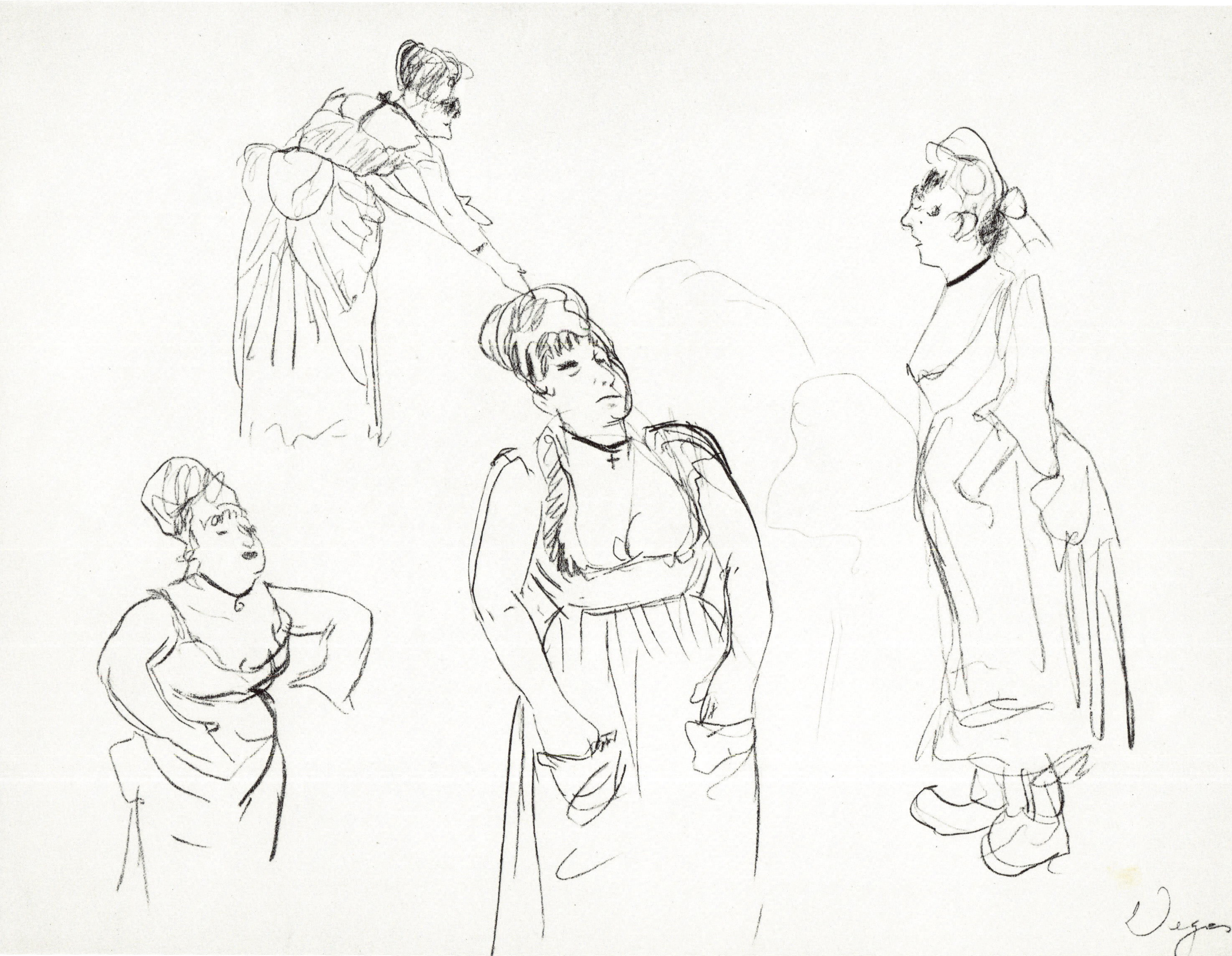
Degas

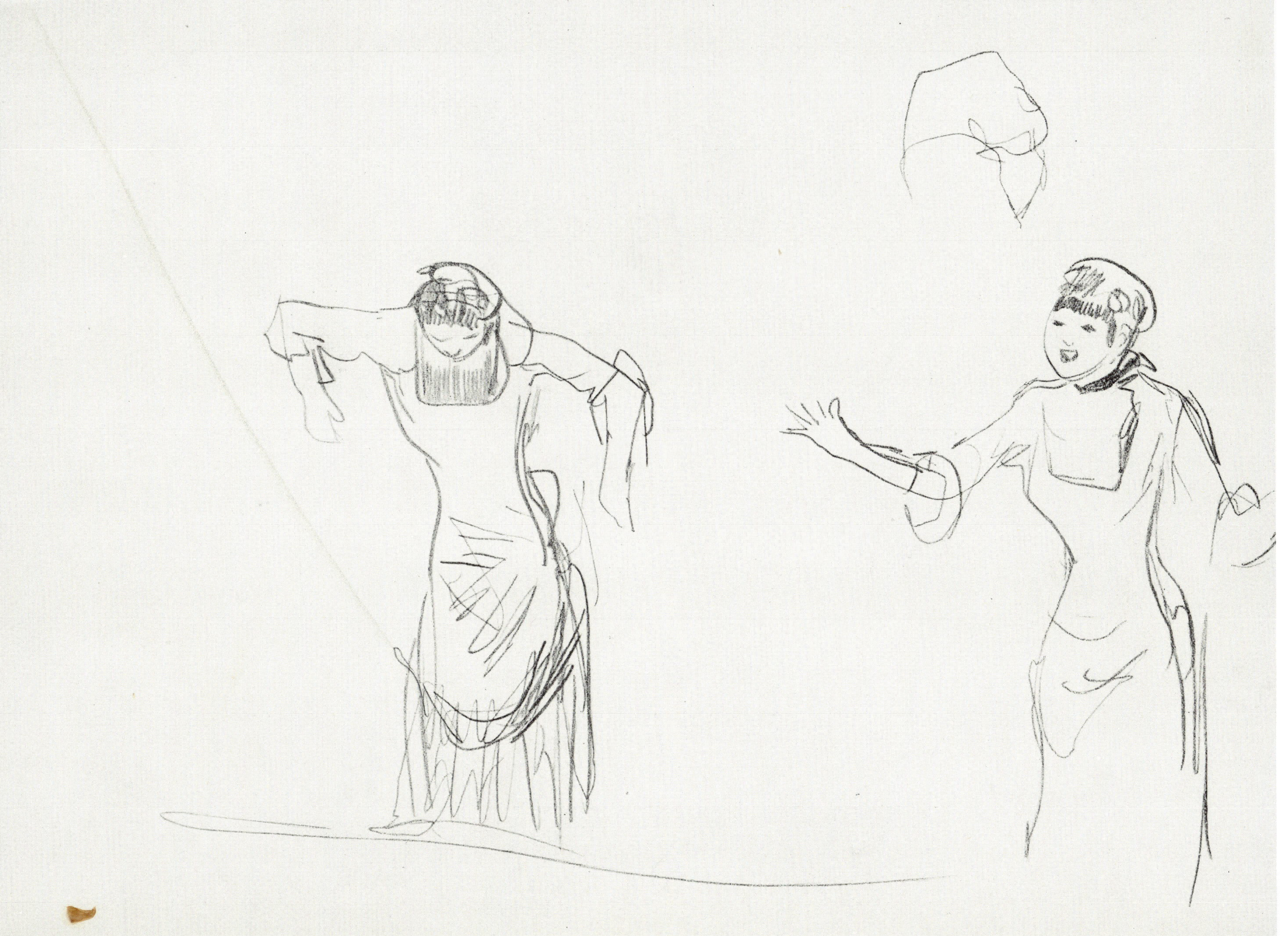

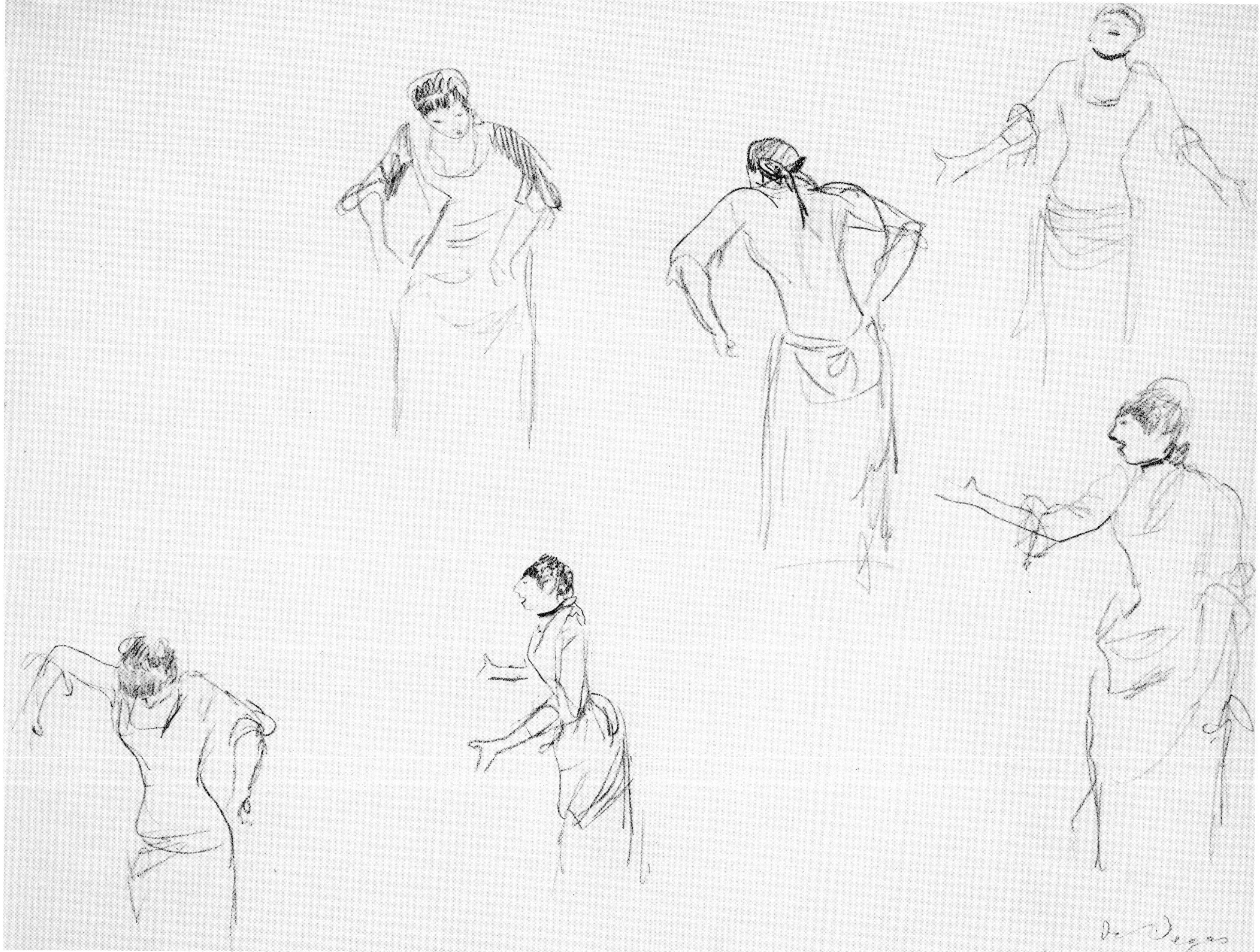

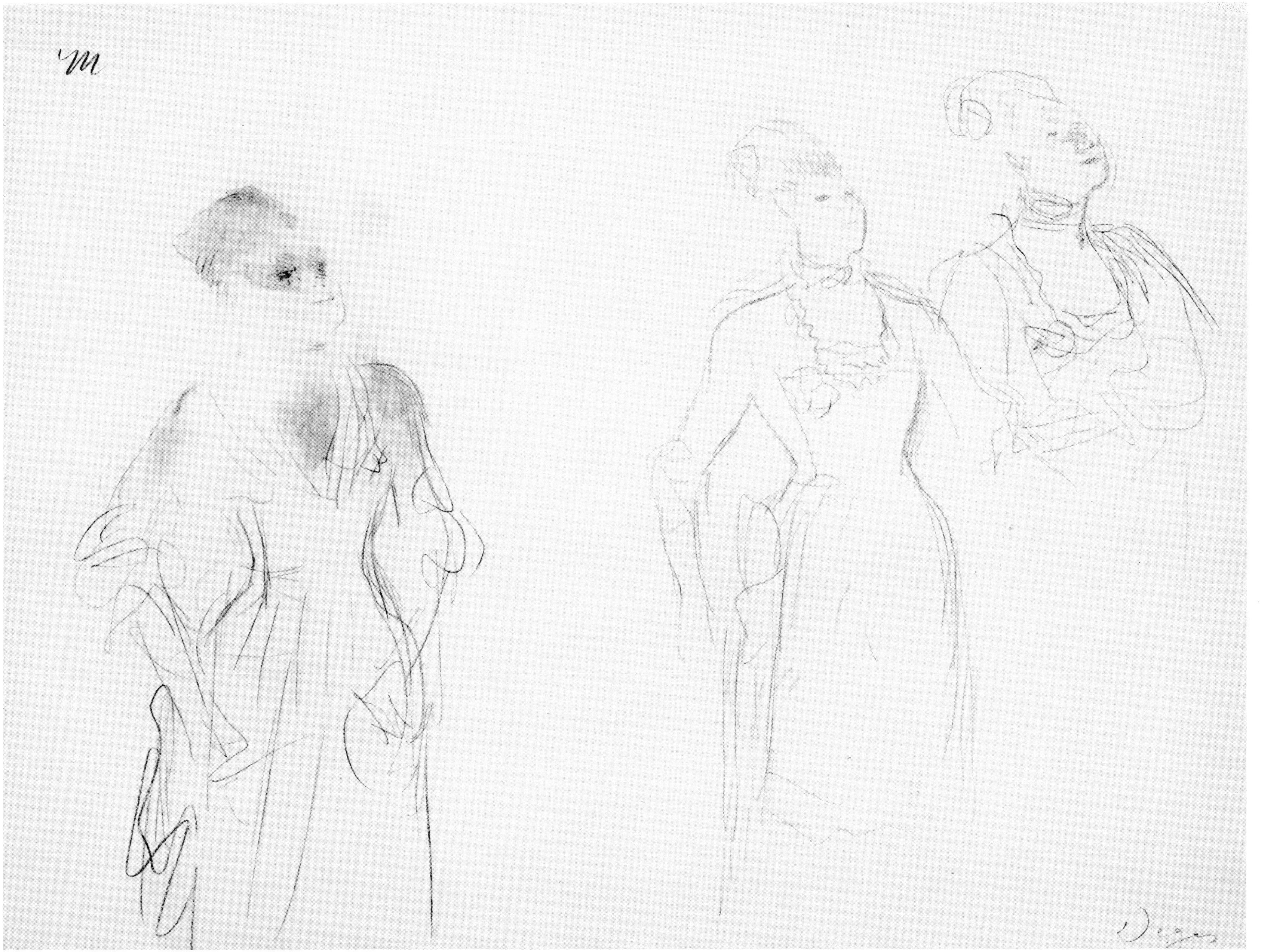

Degas

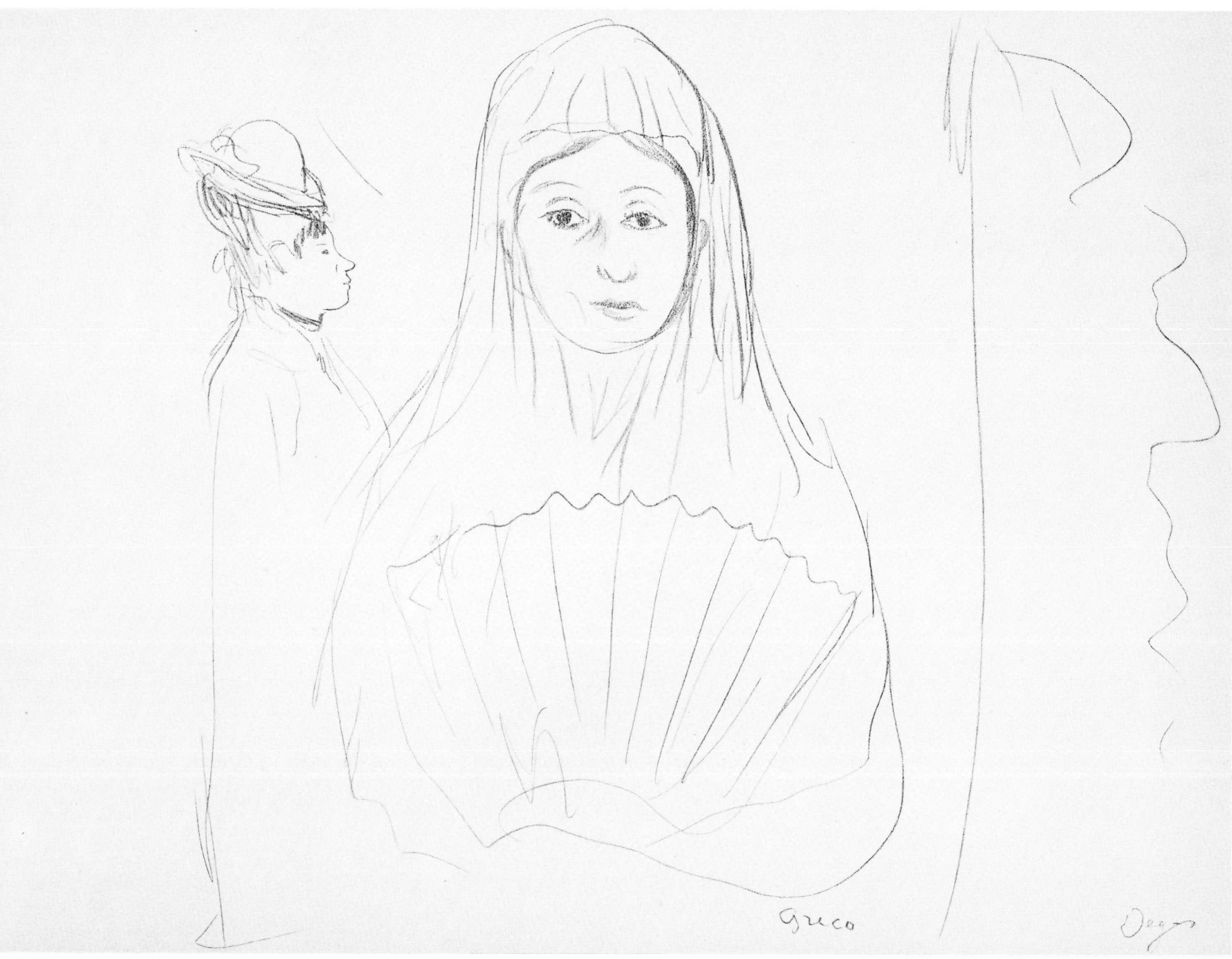
Greco
Degas

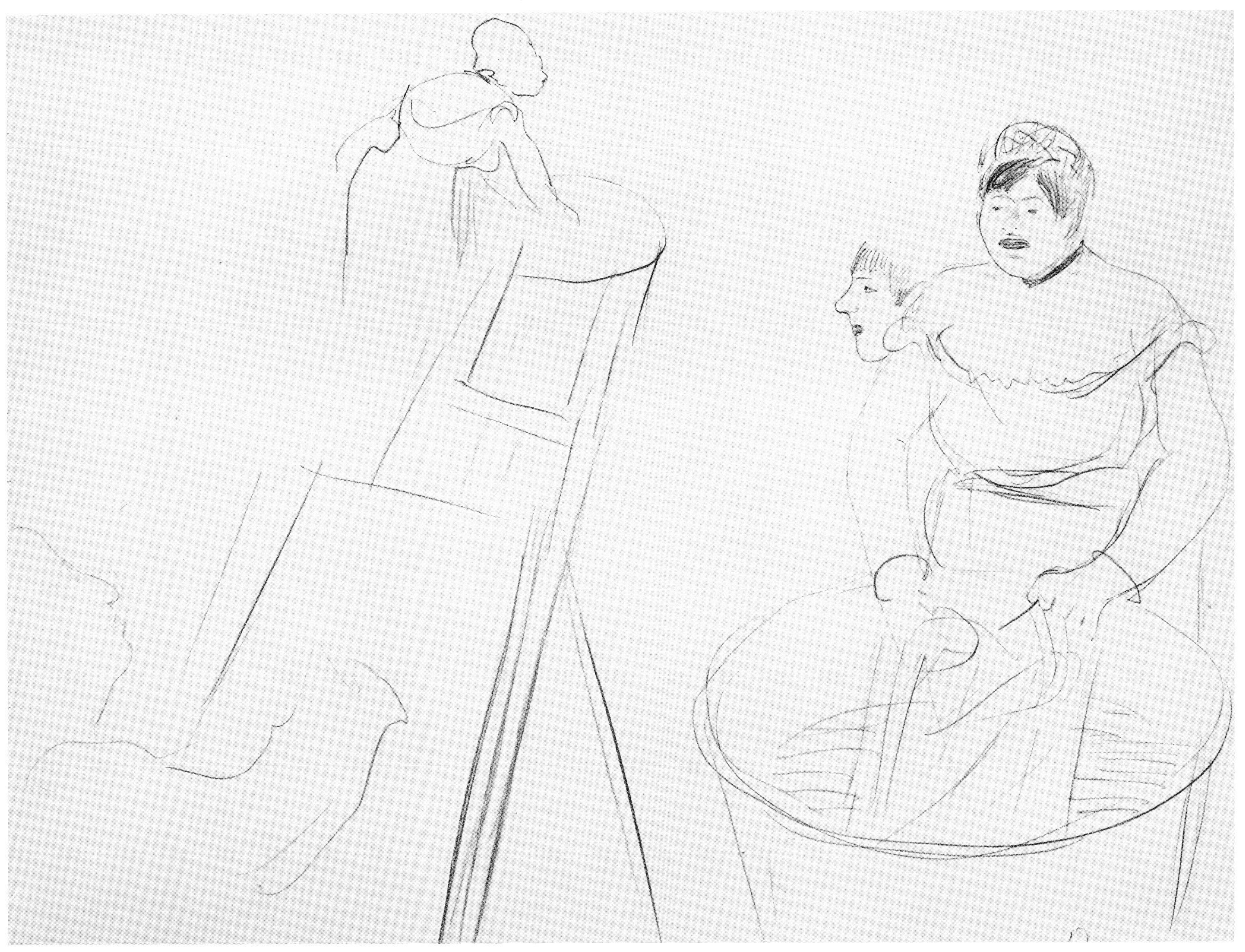

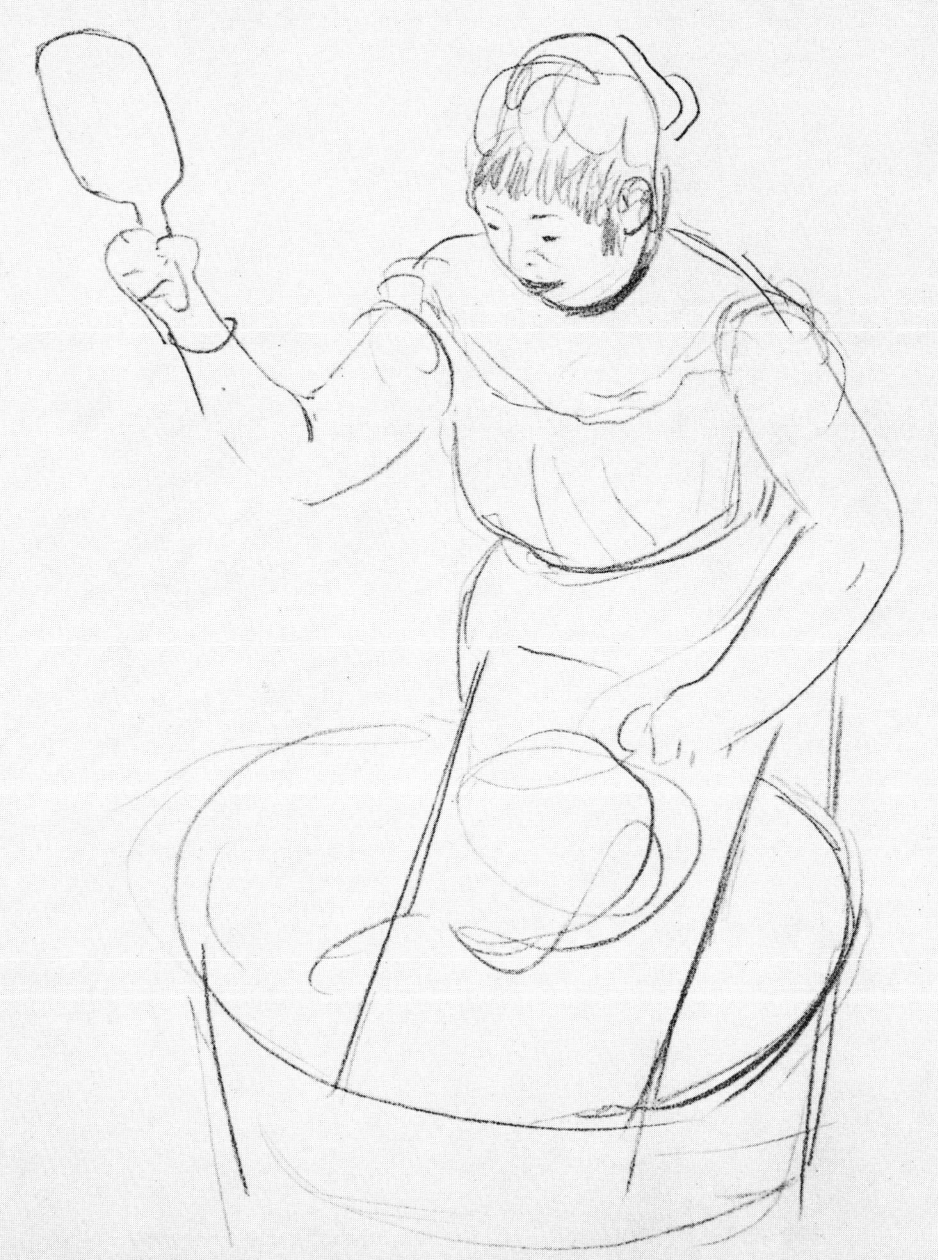

Degas

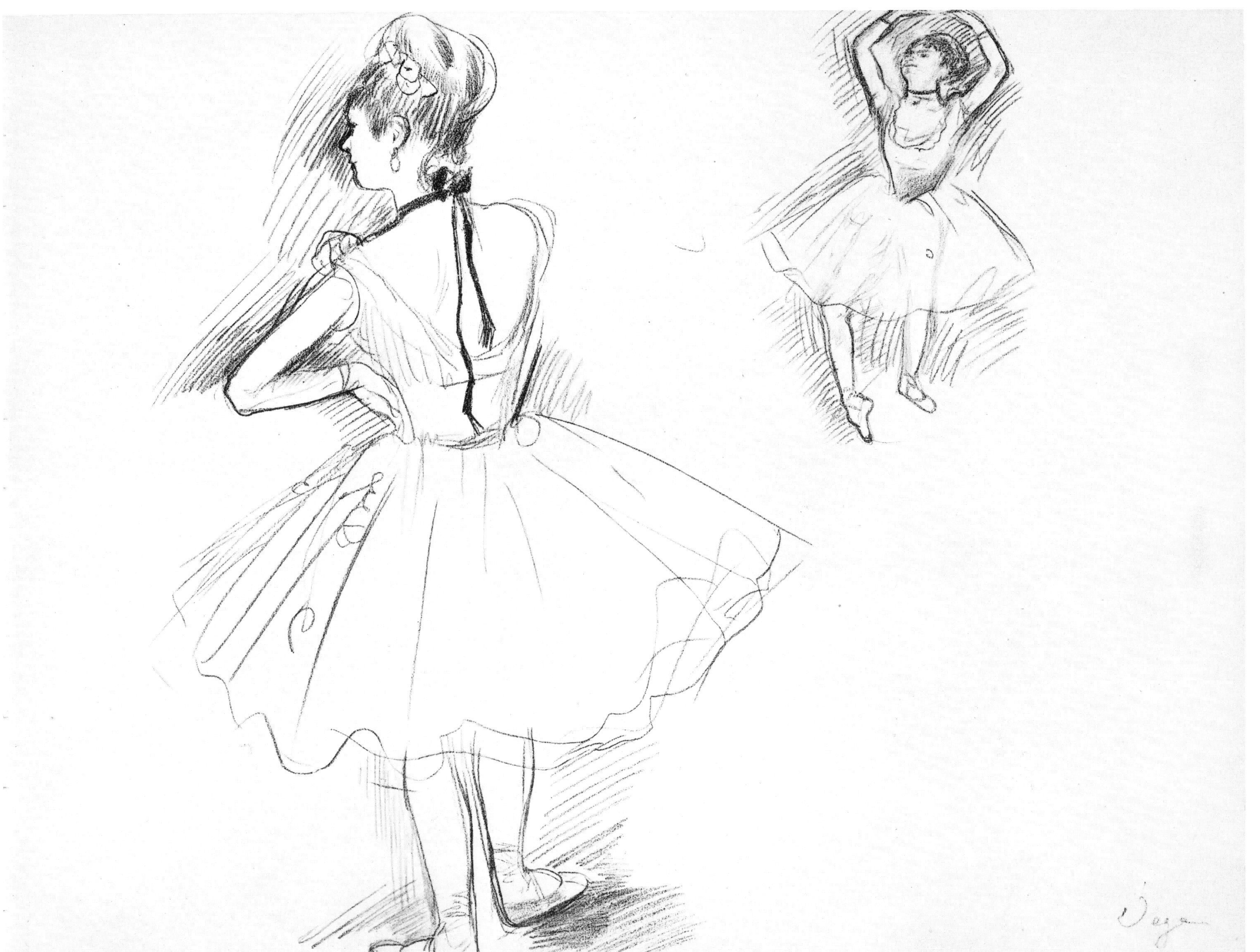
Degas

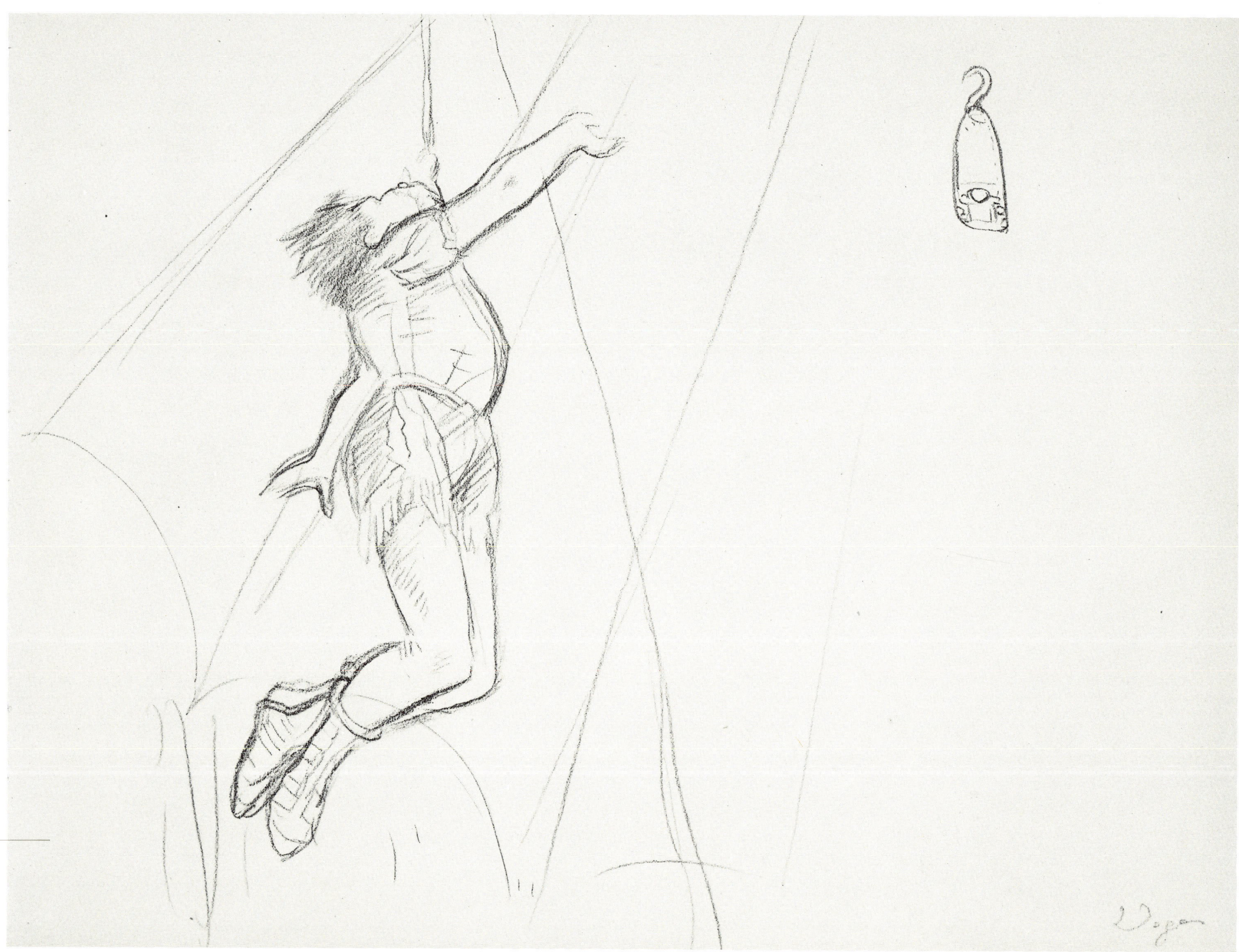

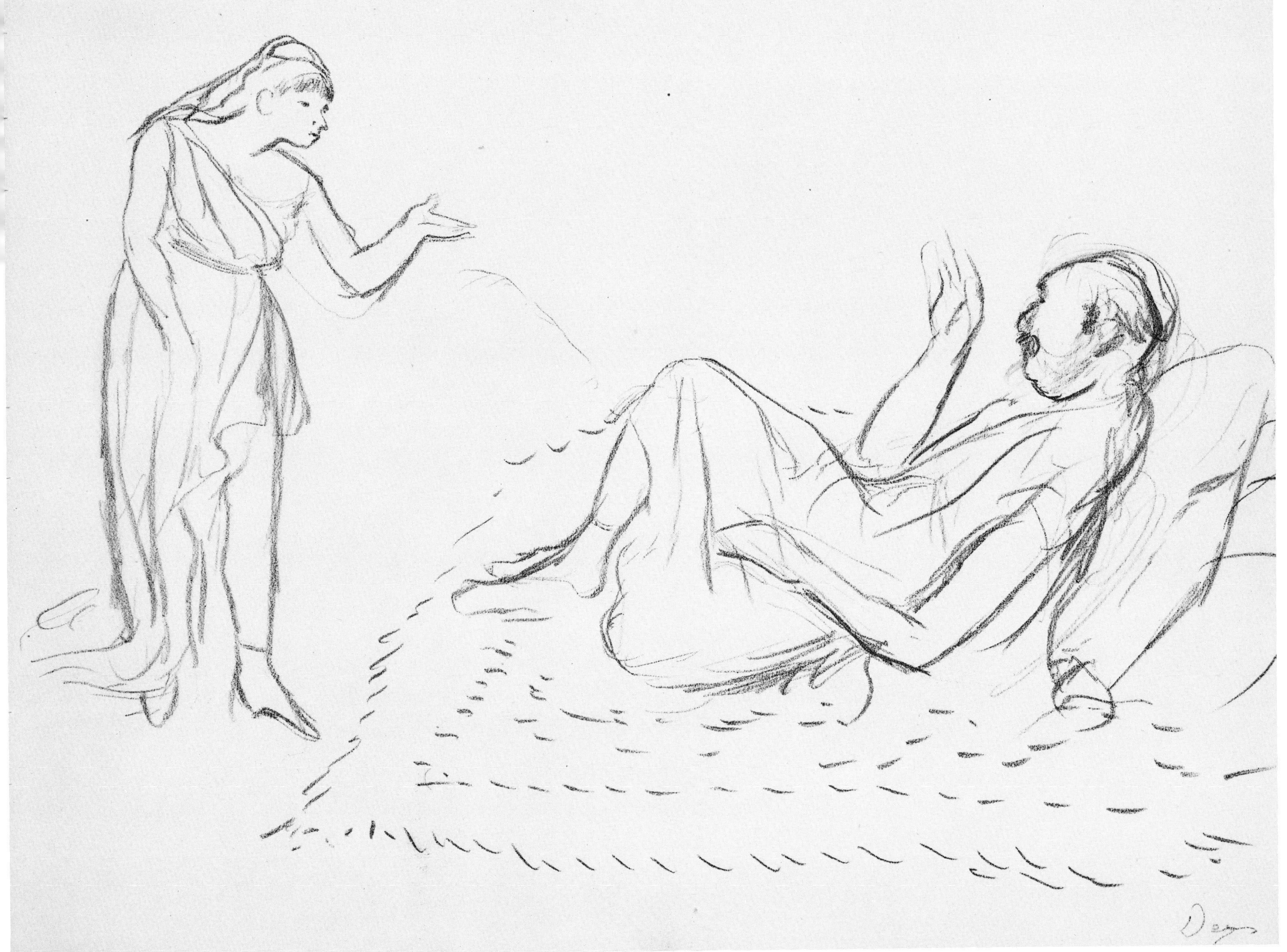

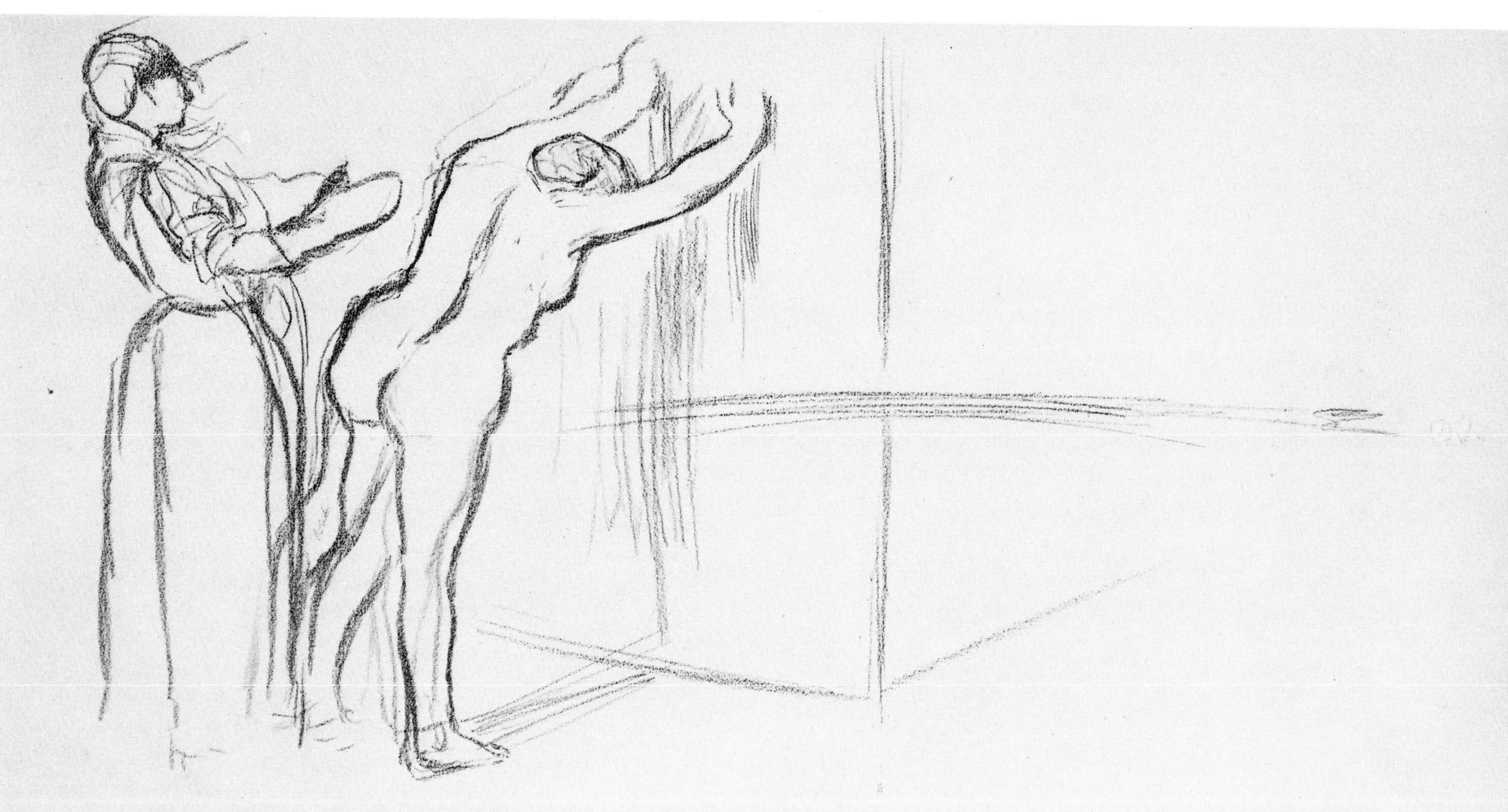

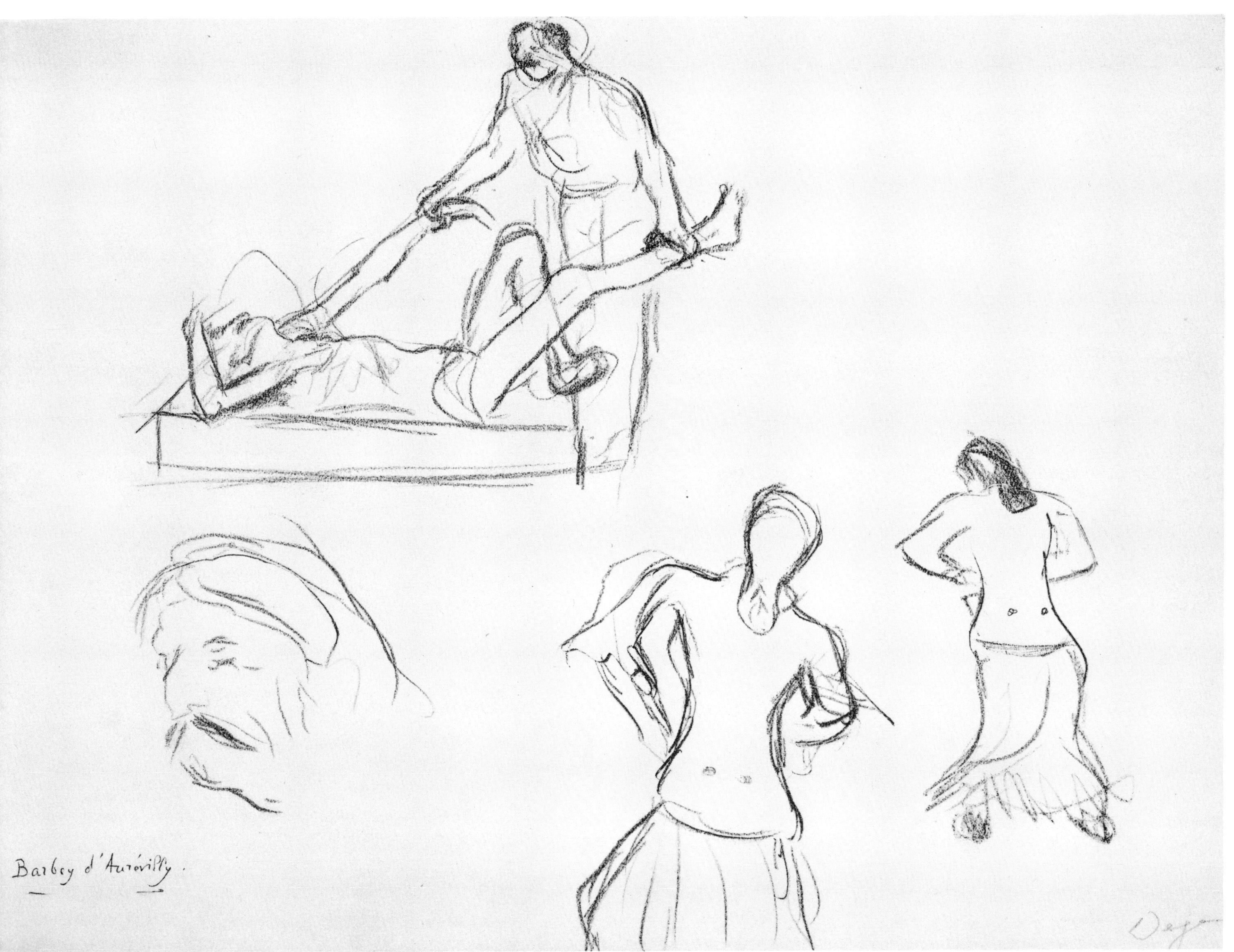
Barbey d'Aurévilly.

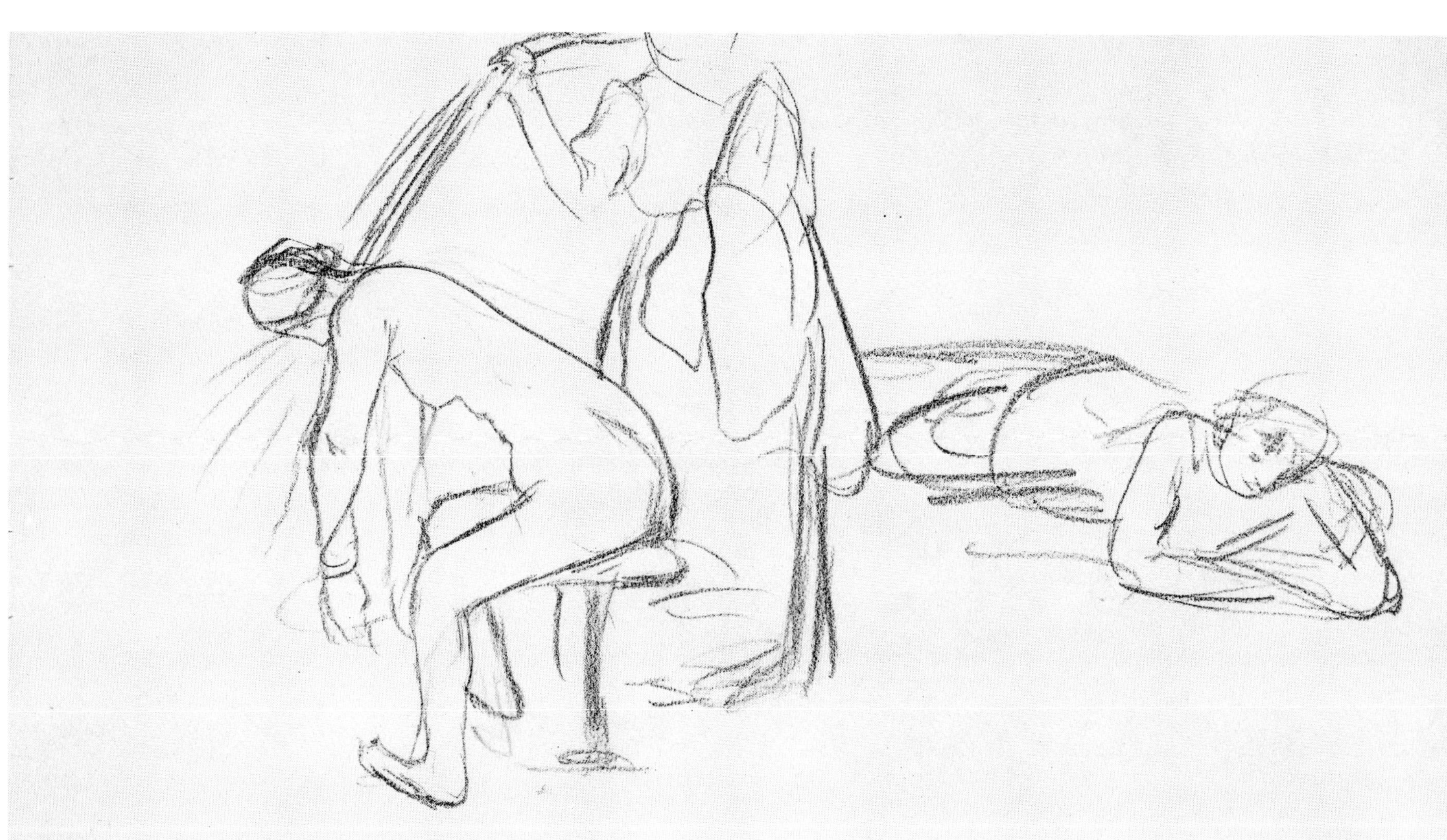

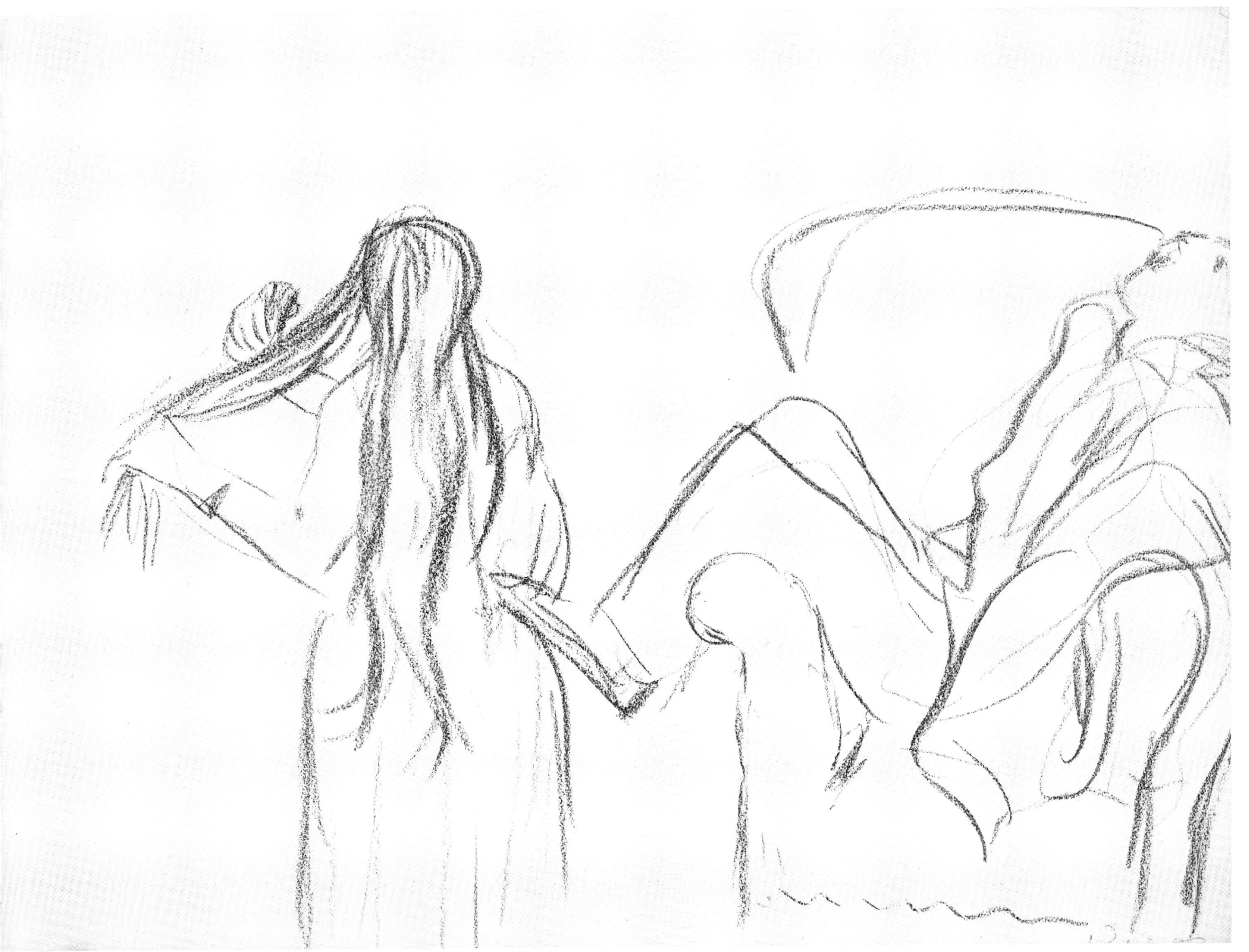

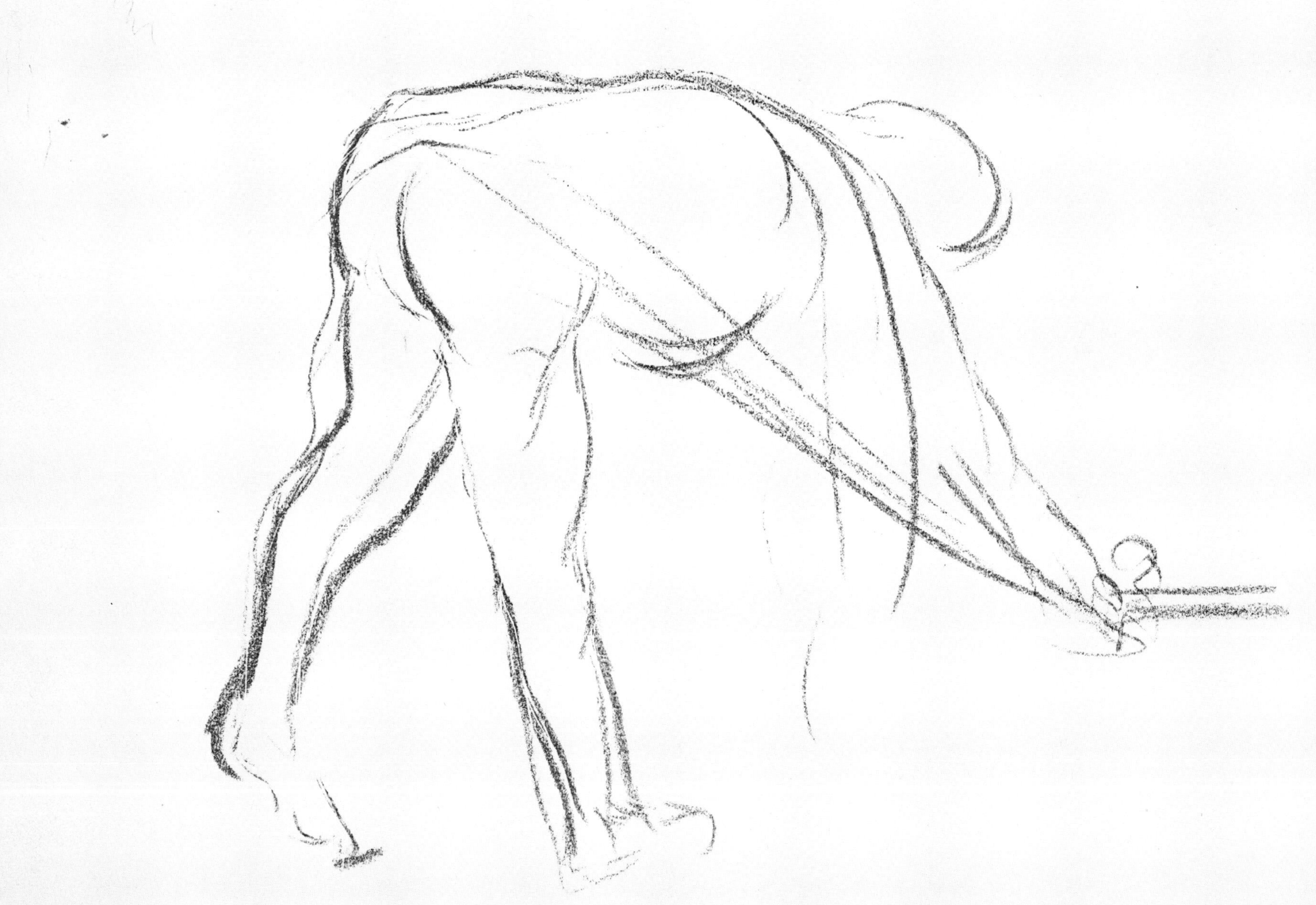
Degas

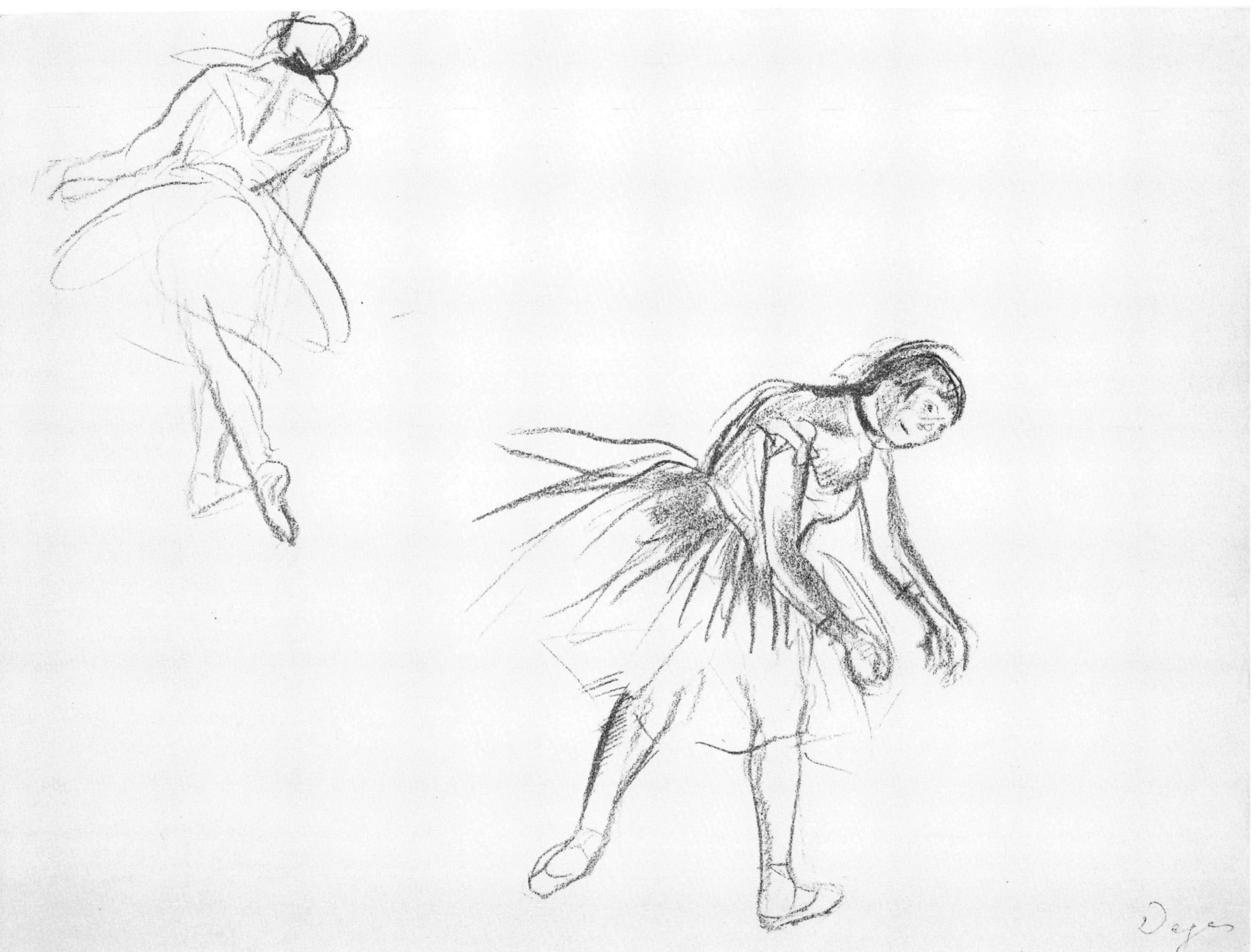

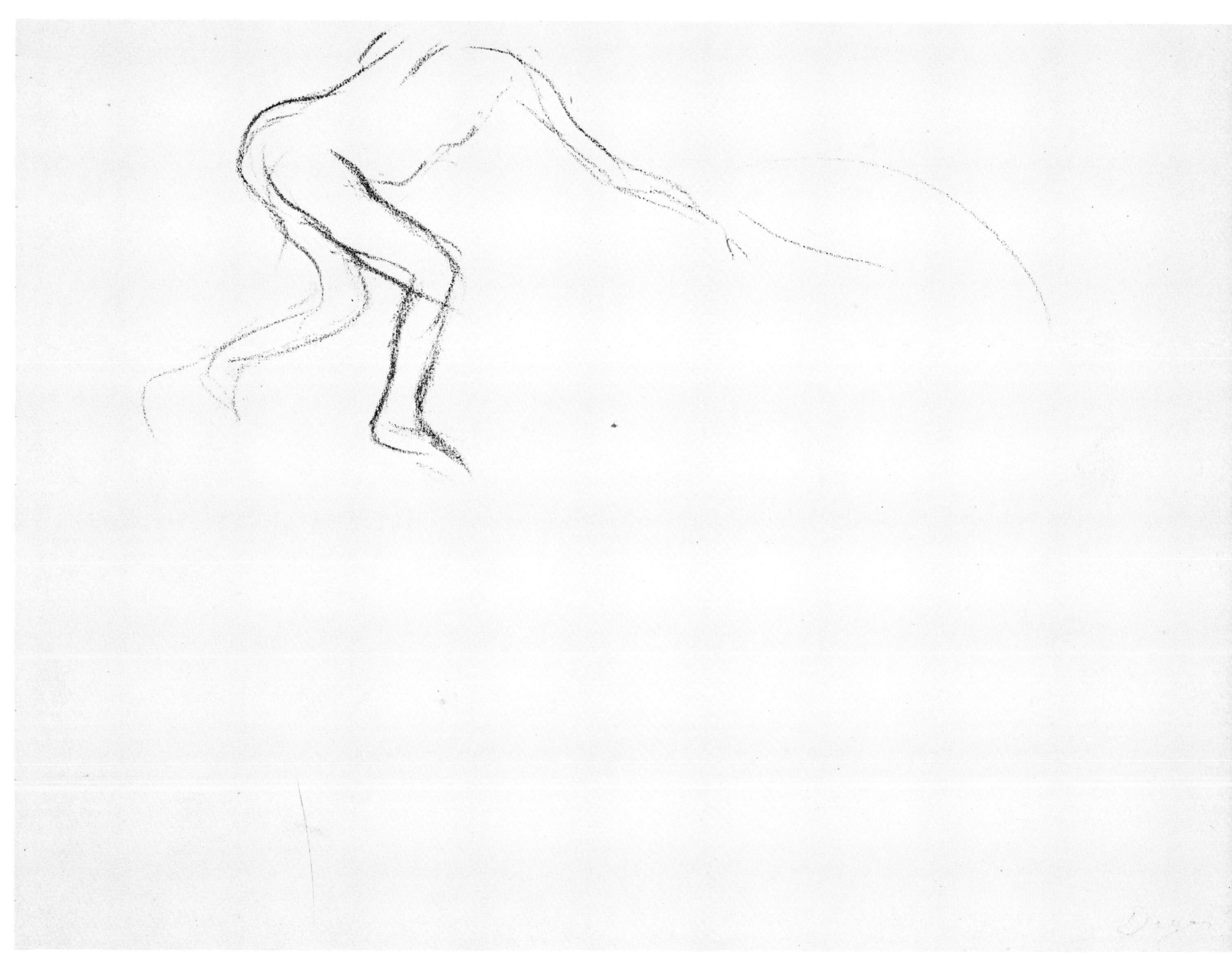